MW00438297

OBAMA'S GLOBE

To Lois

If I could write
everything I feel about you,
it would be a much bigger book
than this one!!

Much Love,
Bruce

OBAMA'S GLOBE

A PRESIDENT'S ABANDONMENT OF U.S. ALLIES AROUND THE WORLD

Bruce Herschensohn

BEAUFORT BOOKS
New York

Map printed with Permission:
The World Factbook 2009. Washington, DC: Central Intelligence Agency, 2012.https://www.cia.gov/library/publications/the-world-factbook/index .html

Library of Congress Cataloging-in-Publication Data

Herschensohn, Bruce, 1932–
 Obama's globe : a president's abandonment of U.S. allies around the world / Bruce Herschensohn.
     p. cm.
Includes bibliographical references.
ISBN 978-0-8253-0685-3 (alk. paper)
1. United States—Foreign relations—2009- 2. Obama, Barack. I. Title.
E907.H47 2012
973.932092—dc23

                                                           2012022183

For inquiries about volume orders, please contact:

Beaufort Books
27 West 20th Street, Suite 1102
New York, NY 10011
sales@beaufortbooks.com

Published in the United States by Beaufort Books
www.beaufortbooks.com

Distributed by Midpoint Trade Books
www.midpointtrade.com

Printed in the United States of America

Interior design by Neuwirth & Associates
Cover Design by Howard Grossman

CONTENTS

PROLOGUE:
AUTHOR'S NOTES

AT THIS WRITING, 1200 days have passed since the day Barack Obama became President of the United States. During those 1200 days the international relations of the United States have changed radically from what had been U.S. foreign policy for decades under Presidents from both major political parties.

This book is not meant to be a complete record of those 1200 days of Barack Obama's presidency but rather a look at those foreign policy changes he initiated that would be difficult to imagine under the administrations of U.S. Presidents Roosevelt, Truman, Eisenhower, Kennedy, Johnson, Nixon, Ford, Reagan, Bush (41), Clinton, and Bush (43) when so much of the world looked for and received the international leadership of the United States. Those were times in which people around the world assumed that Presidents of the United States would treat the U.S.A.'s friends as friends and adversaries as adversaries.

The major stops around the globe in this book are those nations that took prominence in the foreign policies he changed during those 1200 days. Dates used are generally on the United States side of the International Date Line. Before touring Obama's globe within the book, and when pertinent throughout, there are historical references that intersect with the current and future. For ease in reading, details that often would be reserved for footnotes referenced by numbers have instead been enclosed in brackets within the text. This is to avoid reference-numbers causing distractions for some readers while causing other readers to repeatedly go back and forth from the page being read to the last pages of the book in search for the appropriate note. They can, instead, be clearly identified by surrounding brackets, allowing them either to be easily read or skipped by will of the individual reader.

In President Obama's 2012 State of the Union Address starting his fourth year in office, he stated: *"The renewal of American leadership can be felt across the globe . . . Our oldest alliances in Europe and Asia are stronger than ever. Our ties to the Americas are deeper. Our iron-clad commitment to Israel's security has meant the closest military cooperation between our two countries in history . . . Anyone who tells you that America is in decline or that our influence has waned, doesn't know what they're talking about."* But the decline was real and America's influence had severely waned, and President Obama's statements concerning places around the globe were inaccurate. In addition, he left out of his foreign policy summary many of the policies he had enacted. Those inaccuracies and absences are the major subjects of this book.

Bruce Herschensohn

May 3, 2012

1

CEREMONIES

ON INAUGURATION DAY 2009, as soon as Barack Obama said *"So help me God"* in his Oath of Office, there came thunderous cheers and applause of ovation from the thousands assembled outside the U.S. Capitol Building to view the inaugural. At that very moment another event of powerful drama took place in view of everyone in the audience while few noticed it because their eyes were fastened on President Obama and on Chief Justice John Roberts who administered the Oath.

That other event was the "Passing of the Football" that was taking place behind the new President and Chief Justice as the military aide of President Bush passed a heavy black leather-covered briefcase to the man standing next to him: the military aide of President Obama.

It was a single gesture of a slight swing of a man's right arm and the release of his hand, leaving the briefcase in the right hand of the man by his side. As in Presidential Inaugurations before this one, it was the visualization of democracy and the peaceful transition of office, as the briefcase that contained nuclear attack options and the means to put the new President's determination into effect should such a decision be necessary. In addition, a frequently changed plastic card with imbedded metal strands called the biscuit would be given to the President for placement in his clothing so that the football without the biscuit would be impotent.

It has never been recorded how the former President, in this case George W. Bush, felt in that first moment in eight years without the football and the biscuit; their loans to him having expired and now on loan to someone else.

And so on Tuesday, January the 20th of 2009, after 12 Noon, the football was passed and the biscuit was surrendered and the Inaugural Address was given and the 21-gun salute was fired and four Ruffles and Flourishes were sounded by drums and bugles and *Hail to the Chief* was played and the luncheon in Statuary Hall of the Capitol was finished and the Inaugural Parade up Pennsylvania Avenue was done and the last dances at the ten Inaugural Balls were over and the Presidential motorcade went through the night streets of D.C. to 1600 Pennsylvania Avenue N.W. and it was finally the first night of Barack Obama's years in the White House.

[When presidential aspirants promise that should they win the office, they will then take particular policy actions on "Day One"—for the most part don't believe them. A President simply won't have the time with all the things prescribed by tradition. What? And miss the parade and the balls?]

On Inauguration night when all that was done, and after hosting a very late White House party, assume that President

Obama did what presidents preceding him had done that first night by walking from the White House residence through the colonnade to the West Wing and into the Oval Office for some familiarity with what would now be his place of work in that center of power. And assume that President Obama slowly turned his new globe of the world on its stem with his eyes scanning the image of one country after another.

The rest requires no assumptions. At this writing, the fourth year of his Presidency is in progress and assumptions can be exchanged from what could have been done for what has been done.

2

THE WORLD AT WAR

SIXTY-NINE YEARS BEFORE Obama's globe, Prime Minister of the United Kingdom Winston Churchill spoke about his nation's policy against the expansionist forces of Adolph Hitler from Germany. It was May the 13th of 1940 when he spoke to members of the House of Commons: "You ask, 'what is our aim?' I can answer with one word: Victory! Victory at all costs! Victory in spite of all terror! Victory however long and hard the road may be, for without victory there is no survival."

The following year, on December the 8th, 1941, the day following the Japanese Empire's attack on Pearl Harbor, President of the United States Franklin Delano Roosevelt spoke to the members of the U.S. Congress: "No matter how long it may take us to overcome this premeditated invasion, the American people in their righteous might will win through to absolute victory."

Advance the calendar to the 21st Century. During the pursuit of gaining the Democrat's nomination for the 2008 presidential election for President of the United States, Senator Barack Obama talked of the Iraq theater in the current war and did not use the word *victory* or *win* but instead he said, "I will *end* the war. Let there be no doubt; I will *end* this war."

But wars are not ended. Wars are won or lost.

Historically and logically, one side walking away from a war that is being fought frees the path for the other side to win. Walking away may interrupt wars for a period of time, but those periods only serve as intermissions before the side that didn't walk away achieves victory.

Barack Obama, of course, won the nomination and won the office of the presidency, and upholding his belief that wars could be ended rather than won or lost, he soon publicly presented timelines to the world. Although Winston Churchill had said in his May 10th, 1940 Address: "No matter how long it may take," Barack Obama projected dates. The United States would leave Iraq's combat zones by August the 31st of 2010 and leave the rest of Iraq by December the 31st of 2011. The United States would begin the withdrawal in Afghanistan in July of 2011 with U.S. combat troops out by the end of 2014. President Obama's first timeline for Afghanistan had been stated in a unique combination of two sentences one after the other at the Military Academy at West Point on December the 1st of 2009: *"As Commander-in-Chief, I have determined that it is in our vital national interest to send an additional 30,000 U.S. troops to Afghanistan. After 18 months, our troops will begin to come home."* His commanders on the ground had recommended a minimum surge of 40,000 troops and no date set for withdrawal.

On June the 22nd of 2011 he said, *"We are meeting our goals. As a result, starting next month, we will be able to remove 10,000 of our troops from Afghanistan by the end of this year and we will bring home a total of 33,000 troops by next summer,* [in 2012] *fully recovering the surge I announced at West Point."*

On May the 1st of 2012, President Obama said, *"Last year we removed 10,000 U.S. troops from Afghanistan. Another 23,000 will leave by the end of the summer. After that, reductions will continue at a steady pace, with more of our troops coming home. And as our coalition agreed, by the end of 2014 the Afghans will be fully responsible for the security of their country."*

It is a well known story that a warlord in Northeast Afghanistan was talking to an American, and the warlord glanced at the watch on the left wrist of the American, and then he looked back up at the American's eyes and said, "You Americans have all the *watches*. But we have all the *time."*

An announced timeline would have been considered treasonous in World War II because the likely scenario would have been that the free world would have lost the war while the Nazis and the Japanese Empire would have waited for the U.S. self-imposed timeline to be reached, then the enemies would have emerged with weapons blazing to seize victory.

The enemy in the newest global war went unmentioned by name from Barack Obama or his administration. The enemy attacks were identified as "Man Caused Disasters" by President Obama's Secretary of Homeland Security, Janet Napolitano. It was as though the administration didn't really know the cause of those who were blowing up people throughout the world. In a strange contortion of definition, the White House, even in its Office of Management and Budget submission for the

FY 2012 Federal Budget, identified U.S. troops in "Overseas Contingency Operations." Clarity was not an objective. When others identified the enemy as Islamist Jihadists or Islamist Fascists or Expansionists of Jihad or Radical Islamists or Islamist Militants, or when both Senator Joseph Lieberman and the former Governor of New Jersey and Co-Chairman of the 9-11 Commission, Thomas Kean used the phrase, "Violent Islamist Extremism", all such phrases were rejected. And there was and is refusal to call it what it is, in favor of resting with the previously mentioned Man Caused Disasters.

Why the hesitancy to call it what it is? If it isn't referred to as a Global War declared by Radical Islamists, a stronger name should be found; not a weaker one. At this writing, Radical Islamists in that Global War have staged massive terrorist attacks in:

Kandahar
And Bali
And London
And Casablanca
And Khobar
And Islamabad
And Jericho
And Nairobi
And Nazareth
And Moscow
And Mindanao
And Amman
And Luxor

And Istanbul
And Madrid
And Aden
And Sharm El Sheikh
And Kampala
And New Delhi
And Dhaka
And Taba
And Beslan
And Netanya
And Mombasa
And Riyadh
And Karachi
And Dar es Salaam
And Aqaba
And Cairo
And Beirut
And Dahab
And Algiers
And Glasgow
And Sanaa
And Rawalpindi
And Mumbai
And Jakarta
And Peshawar
And Maiduguri
And Alexandria
And Mosul
And Abuja

And, of course, New York City and the Pentagon in Arlington, Virginia, and because of courageous actions of passengers, not the U.S. Capitol Building which was targeted, but a rural area of Somerset County in Pennsylvania.

Radical Islamist terrorist groups were and remain headquartered around the world, [most prominently al-Qaeda and Lashkar-e-Taiba in Pakistan; Boko Haram in Nigeria; Ansar Dine in Mali, Abu Sayyaf in the Philippines, al-Shabaab in Somalia; Hezbollah in Lebanon; Hamas in the Gaza Strip; Ansar al-Sharia in Yemen formerly known as A.Q.A.P., al-Qaeda in the Arabian Peninsula; Indian Mujahideen in India; the Taliban and the Haqqani Network in both Afghanistan and Pakistan, and a minimum of 54 more organizations,] some with foreign or home-grown cells in Europe, Asia, Latin America, and the United States.

The word "terrorism" was occasionally used by the administration but without any prefix, and when challenged for not being identified, the answer was that terrorism has also been committed by those who are not Radical Islamists but even committed by *Americans*: "For example, there was the 1995 bombing of the Murrah Federal Building in Oklahoma City and the 2011 shooting of Congresswoman Gabrielle Giffords."

But those were criminal acts; not a concerted and armed world-wide theological and political pursuit to expand an ideology over nations of the world. Another difference was that in the cases of the tragedies of Oklahoma City and the shooting of Congresswoman Giffords there were no celebrations in American cities but only grief, whereas throughout many Arab and other Islamic cities, the tragedy of 9-11, as well as other terrorist attacks, brought celebrations.

When the Fort Hood massacre was committed [November the 5th of 2009] by Army Major Nidal Hasan, members of the Obama Administration and many media voices told Americans not to judge too quickly the motivation of Major Hassan. Good advice if so much wasn't already known. He was called "a lone wolf" although he called out *Allahu Akbar* before he pulled the trigger each time, killing 13 and wounding or injuring 42 others; although he carried business cards in which he called himself *Soldier of Allah*. and he had exchanged as many as 20 emails with Anwar al-Awlaki, the leader of al-Qaeda in the Arabian Peninsula located in Yemen.

The official Department of Defense report did not associate Nidal Hasan with Islam. Senator Susan Collins, with justifiable anger, produced a letter from the Department of Defense in which Nidal's killings were referred to as "workplace violence."

Away from home, President Obama frequently called the battlefields of Iraq and Afghanistan *"two wars."* During his presidential campaign at a rally in New Mexico [August the 18th of 2008] he said of Iraq, *"It was a war of choice, not a war of necessity."* As President in his speech at Cairo University [June the 5th of 2009] when speaking of Afghanistan, he said, *"We did not go by choice, we went because of necessity . . . Unlike Afghanistan, Iraq was a war of choice . . . "* It was a kind of good-war and bad-war since at that time giving argument against the U.S. fighting in Afghanistan would have given justification to those who had accused the leadership of the Democrats as still being opposed to the use of the military as they had been accused since 1972 when George McGovern ran for the presidency with the slogan of isolationism: "Come Home, America."

To the United Nations General Assembly [September the 21st of 2011] he said, *"I took office at a time of two wars for the United States."* And so "two wars" were continued to be the common call of Iraq and Afghanistan. But World War II was known as a World War; not the Germany War, the Italy War, the France War, the Japan War, the Philippine War, the Midway Island War, the Wake Island War, the Casablanca War, the Algiers War, and other wars. Those were battles within theaters of the war: the European Theater and the Pacific Theater and the Mediterranean (North Africa) and Middle Eastern Theater. When the United States and its allies fought in France, that fight and liberation was part of the European Theater. The fight and liberation of the Philippines were part of the Pacific Theater as were Midway and Wake Island. And when the United States and its allies fought in Algeria it was part of the Mediterranean and Middle Eastern Theater. To define the zones of military action as battlefields within theaters of one war—a World War—was and is important because that serves as a consistent reminder that all theaters must be won to achieve victory.

It is therefore likely that President Obama never saw the globe of the world in the way that President Franklin Delano Roosevelt and Harry S. Truman saw their Oval Office globes when facing the axis powers during the years of World War II. Admittedly and understandably he didn't live through it, but it is imperative that he and all future Presidents know the elements that brought the United States to be victorious in what appeared, at first, to be unwinnable.

In World War II the United States and its allies bombed the enemy to blazes without restraint and into submission from

Dresden to Hamburg to Berlin and from Kobe to Osaka to Tokyo. After the costly allied invasion of Europe with immense casualties, the atomic bomb was ready and to prevent a need for an invasion of Japan, it was used on Hiroshima and Nagasaki.

In that war, rules of engagement did not call for government lawyers to be contacted to find out if bombing targets of enemies must be cancelled because civilians may be present within those targets.

At home during World War II American civilians were just as distant from political correctness as their counterparts in the Armed Forces: their victory was not achieved by giving false accusations against the United States for being in the war; it was not achieved by calling for an end of domestic profiling; it was not achieved by demonstrating against our military involvement. There was not the illogical statement that "I support the troops but oppose their mission." By that standard they could as easily have supported the troops of the *enemy* while opposing *their* mission. That phrase of supporting the troops but opposing their mission originated from guilt of those who did *not* support U.S. troops in Vietnam, [some having given cat-calls and even spit on those in uniform who returned] and so later, when condemning troops became unpopular, devised an irrational phrase to save themselves by separating troops from their mission. But it didn't hold up because a person is synonymous with his or her mission. It is not said that people support nurses but not their mission, or support carpenters but not their mission, or support airline pilots but not their mission, or support teachers but not their mission.

Almost every American, military or civilian during World War II took pride in living their missions. Some at home became "Rosie the Riveter" and Air Raid Wardens and other essential *missions*. They wanted to devote themselves to victory, and that devotion was accomplished by taking part in the war as an every-day event. At home, gasoline was rationed with black "A", blue "B", and green "C" stickers on windshields of cars signifying how much gasoline the owner of the car could buy. The purchase of shoes called for shoe-stamps. The material of those shoes available was synthetic. Cash alone was not enough to purchase most foods as they were sold with ever-present rationing books and different colored stamps and chips. Victory Gardens of vegetables and fruits were grown at home. War Chest Campaigns were frequent "for our Armed Forces and for our allies. Have you given your share?" All that had to be known was that it was for the war effort.

There was not a simultaneous cry for saving the environment and there was no demand for creating higher paying jobs or an insistence on government provided health-care. All subjects other than victory were nothing more than luxury during the war.

Most important, there was no demand by the people for an exit strategy and there was no exit strategy given by President Roosevelt other than one word: Victory. That word meant the absolute and unconditional surrender of the enemies of the United States. No negotiations. No deals. No power-sharing. No acceptance of enemy-led political parties in governmental coalitions in their home countries. No compromises.

The mission was even engaged by the children of those years as there were paper-drives in schools which meant the students would bring a week's worth of newspapers to their school's playground to be shipped to processing factories making cartons for war supplies. And there were scrap drives where students brought to school any pieces of metal for the war effort. Mothers saved grease from their frying pans and their children brought the precious cargo to school for the war effort. From empty cigarette packs of their parents or scavenged, children would separate the pack's tin foil from its backing-paper, roll the tin foil into a ball, and turn it in for the war effort. The prestige of the time was when the ball was huge, to envelope it in wrappers of "Old Gold" cigarettes because the tin-foil was gold rather than silver and created a more precious looking ball. When they could, the student's parents gave children a dime to buy a stamp to put in their United States Defense Savings Bonds Album that stated, "When you fill this album with one-hundred eighty-seven 10 cent stamps and add 5 cents in coin, it will have a total value of $18.75 which will buy a Defense Savings Bond at your nearest post office worth, in 10 years, $25.00."

Out of such unity, the generation's *pursuit* of victory led to the *achievement* of victory. And that generation is today accurately known as what Tom Brokaw called the Greatest Generation.

That is how World War II was won.

It was how, on the first day of September 1945, while General Macarthur was accepting the surrender of the Japanese Empire on the battleship U.S.S. Missouri, President Truman was able to say in a radio broadcast to the world: "Four years ago, the thoughts and fears of the whole civilized world were centered on another piece of American soil—Pearl Harbor. The mighty threat to civilization which began there is now laid to rest. It was a long road to Tokyo—and a bloody one . . . This is a victory of more than arms alone. This is a victory over tyranny . . . Back of it all were the will and spirit and determination of a free people who know what freedom is, and who know that it is worth whatever price they had to pay to preserve it."

And then came an unprecedented action of a victor. The United States could easily have made the world its taxpayer but, instead, the United States had the unique character not to even think of such a course. Rather the United States chose to charge its own citizens for the rebuilding of both friendly nations and nations of former foes starting with the Marshall Plan as well as aid programs in the Far East.

But when President Obama was asked by Ed Luce of the *Financial Times* if he believed in American exceptionalism [April the 4th of 2009], President Obama answered, *"I believe in American exceptionalism just as I suspect that the Brits believe in British exceptionalism and the Greeks believe in Greek exceptionalism."*

Later, he told Steve Kroft on CBS' *60 Minutes* [November the 9th of 2011], *"I would put our legislative and foreign policy accomplishments in our first two years against any President, with the possible exceptions of Johnson, FDR and Lincoln, just in terms of what we've gotten done in modern history."*

In the Global War against Radical Islamists there has been consistent effort to nation-build and win the hearts and minds while at war. That was not done in the 1940s until *after* the war was won. There was recognition that winning hearts and minds by nation-building could not be done while bombing their nations. Nation-building and winning hearts and minds were reserved for a latter time after victory was achieved.

President Obama might have considered telling the American people what could happen if the war was lost. Instead his administration cast it in this way: That "when we leave" we could then use the billions of dollars that would have continued to be spent on the military, for the building of our schools and for the cleaning of our environment and for the maintenance of our infrastructure, and for a litany of those things here at home. It is true that much of that could then be done if U.S. budgets permitted, but it is likely that in that kind of future, the United States would be building and accomplishing those things so they could be approved and directed by an Ayatollah or a Mullah or a Sheik or an Imam under the imposition of strict Sharia law. That is because if the war was not won, it would be lost.

And Novembers of even-numbered years in future times would then pass without the nuisance of elections.

3

THE STUFF OF PRESIDENTS

The Stuff of Presidents is not an original statement made here, but plagiarized from something that happened in the Oval Office of the White House in April of 1961 after President Kennedy had ordered the covert invasion of Cuba into the Bay of Pigs. In view of the invasion's terrible conclusion, he asked former Vice President Nixon to the Oval Office to discuss foreign policy, having known first-hand his guest's expertise in foreign affairs from their years together in the United States Congress.

Former Vice President Nixon was sitting on a lounge chair in the Oval Office while President Kennedy was pacing back and forth over the office's carpet, and they discussed the world conflicts of the time: Cuba, West Berlin, the Congo, Egypt under Nasser, the continuing battles between Pakistan and India over Kashmir, Laos, South Vietnam, the tensions between Sukarno of Indonesia and the United Nations, and so it went as the conversation went around the globe from one place to another.

After that long discussion, President Kennedy stopped pacing and there was silence as the President stared at the former Vice President. And then President Kennedy said, "This is the stuff of Presidents, isn't it?"

Former Vice President Nixon gave a slight smile and nodded.

President Kennedy then gave statements about the President's authority over foreign affairs and, in contrast, how the Congress is needed for determination of most domestic and economic issues. He gave as illustration the then-current debate over whether or not the minimum wage should be raised one dime an hour from $1.15 to $1.25. He knew he had more authority to retain or raise the minimum wage when he was a Congressman or a Senator than he did as President. All he could do as President was advocate his position but not appropriate. Although he was able to convince the Congress on that one, he was unable to win on legislation regarding a number of policy advocacies, and most of all he was unable to convince the Congress to pass his major tax reductions and civil rights legislation, neither of which he was able to get passed through the Congress while he was President. [It wasn't until after his assassination in 1963 that both passed as 1964 Acts of the Congress and signed by President Lyndon Baines Johnson.]

But on foreign policy it was different. He was Commander in Chief. He was solely responsible for the failure in the outcome of the Bay of Pigs invasion, and later was solely responsible for the success in the outcome of the Cuban Missile Crisis. The Congress had no role in either one. Those decisions and outcomes were the stuff of Presidents.

Seven Presidents after President Kennedy, President Clinton couldn't get his health care plan through the Congress. But when he wanted the U.S. military to intervene in Bosnia and Kosovo and Haiti, the military intervened. Following President Clinton, President Bush (43) couldn't get Congress to pass his Social Security Reform or Immigration Reform. But when he wanted the U.S. military to go into Afghanistan and Iraq, he did it. And when President Obama followed him into office, the new President wanted his own health-care plan put into law. His comfortable majority in the 111th Congress eventually voted for it but it took him a year to get it through passage of the Congress and without a single-payer system. But when he wanted to give timelines for the U.S. military to leave Iraq and Afghanistan, he just ordered them. And when he wanted the U.S. military to intervene in Libya and then put NATO rather than the United States in charge of the action, he just did it.

For sure, the Congress has influence with the President and the President has influence with the Congress and both have influence with the public, but when it comes to resolution of policies, with little exception the Congress has the final word on *domestic* matters, while with little exception *foreign* policy decisions are, as President Kennedy called them, "the stuff of Presidents." Or as President George W. Bush was to say [during a controversy with the press as he voiced confidence in his Secretary of Defense against critics] "Mine is the final decision . . . I'm the decider."

[Presidents must seek the Senate's advice and consent for Treaties but often Presidents avoid that by making Executive Agreements or Accords with foreign governments rather than Treaties. Also Presidents must seek the Senate's advice and consent for appointments of U.S. Ambassadors but in the case of rejection of a nominee, Presidents either nominate someone else the President feels has a similar judicial philosophy, or the one rejected can be and have been appointed during a period of Senate recess. The President's foreign *policies* remain intact.]

Although the Constitution gives the authority to the Congress for declarations of war, there have been only five such declarations in U.S. history while there have been over 240 U.S. foreign military operations under the constitutional authority of the President as Commander in Chief. [The five declared wars were the War of 1812, the Mexican-American War, the Spanish-American War, World War I and World War II. Even in FDR's request to the Congress regarding the attack on Pearl Harbor in which a vote was taken, that request was worded by him not as a U.S. declaration of war but, instead, that the war *has existed* by the wording, "I ask that the Congress declare that since the unprovoked and dastardly attack by Japan on Sunday, December the Seventh, a state of war has existed between the United States and the Japanese Empire." That day, the Eighth of December, Japan issued a formal declaration of war against the United States and the British Empire.]

Historically, disregarding personal issues or scandals or assassination, the events that most instantly come to mind regarding Presidents since the United States became the world's leading international power, are generally issues of foreign policy, overtaking domestic issues: Truman with the Atom Bomb; Eisenhower with the cease-fire in Korea; Kennedy with the Cuban Missile Crisis; Johnson with Vietnam; Nixon with Vietnam and opening the door to China; Ford for no particular policy either foreign or domestic; Carter with the Iranian Hostage Crisis; Reagan with "Mr. Gorbachev, Tear Down This Wall!"; Bush (41) with the Liberation of Kuwait; Clinton for no particular policy either foreign or domestic [coming into office after the Cold War was won and before 9-11 occurred]; and Bush (43) with the military interventions in Afghanistan and Iraq.

Constitutional procedure dictates that in most *domestic* affairs, even when a President opposes some bill that originates in the Congress, the Congress can pass the bill. The President, of course, can refuse to sign it, vetoing the bill, but the Congress can override the President's veto and the President is out of constitutional means as he cannot veto their override. The Congress therefore has the *domestic* policy role of "decider."

Nothing proved the point of congressional preeminence in domestic affairs overriding the President as convincingly as President Obama's speech to a Joint Session of the Congress on September the 8th of 2011 when he literally begged the members of the Congress to pass his "American Jobs" bill. If nothing else, his repeated appeal within that speech was a public admission that the Congress was needed for its passage. Some excerpts of the speech in the order in which they occurred were: *"I am sending this Congress a plan that you should pass right away . . . You should pass this jobs plan right away . . . Pass this jobs bill—pass this jobs bill . . . Pass this jobs bill . . . You should pass it right away . . . You should pass it right away . . . Pass this jobs bill . . . Pass this bill . . . Pass this jobs bill . . . Pass this bill . . . Pass this jobs bill . . . Pass this jobs bill . . . Pass this bill right away . . . Regardless of the arguments we've had in the past, regardless of the arguments we'll have in the future, this plan is the right thing to do right now. You should pass it."* They passed parts of it. Even those parts took Congress nearly seven months. [April the 5th of 2012.]

Those separate final authorities of the President and the Congress regarding foreign and domestic policies are factors that most presidential hopefuls either don't know or ignore in their campaigns. Added to this is that so many major news analysts either don't know or rarely mention it to their readers, listeners, and viewers. Most unfortunate of all is that most voters are left unaware of what a President and a Congress can do—and what they cannot do, but can only advocate.

In the long 2011–2012 series of debates by Republican Presidential aspirants facing state caucuses and primaries, by far most questions asked were concerning issues over which those answering would not have control should they become President. Most questions and subsequent answers were, in fact, a waste of time, and worse than a waste of time, created an impression to voters that a President would have the power to do all things discussed in those debates. This was not unique to that presidential election period alone, but normal for most presidential election periods.

Out of it all, elected Presidents often come into office with grand plans for domestic affairs having given too little emphasis to foreign policy. For a while most presidents fight the constitutionally obvious and the historically confirmed, but eventually most of them make the transition to reality before it is too late and most of them have faced reality well. But not all of them.

4

THE CARTER EXAMPLE

BEFORE TOURING OBAMA'S globe, it is worth noting that the greatest accomplishment of the Jimmy Carter Presidency was that he provided forthcoming Presidents with the evidence of what tremendous damage could be done by choosing to abandon the nation's friends. Studying his record would be worth the time of any new President. [No new President should leave it up to the State Department for an education on foreign policy. There are things that those at the State Department want a new President to know and things they do not want a new President to know.]

Shortly after becoming President, Jimmy Carter advocated a Human Rights Campaign against international violators. To most Americans there was the assumption he would level that campaign toward Leonid Brezhnev of the Soviet Union or Fidel Castro of Cuba or Kim Il-sung of North Korea. But that wasn't what he had in mind. Instead, he moved against friends of the United States who although were authoritarian leaders, none of them were totalitarians or expansionists. First came Humberto Romero of El Salvador and Anastasio Somoza of Nicaragua and then others who, like Romero and Somoza, supported the United States in the Cold War.

Near the beginning of Humberto Romero's administration of El Salvador, the government security forces were accused of killing 40 demonstrators. And so President Carter cut off all aid to El Salvador. That had never been done to El Salvador in the past. *All* aid stopped. With the United States out of the picture, communist guerrillas known as the FMLN [the Farabundo Marti Liberation Nacional] escalated what had been occasional attacks into a war to take over El Salvador. Romero was overthrown and replaced by a Carter supported junta.

Next door in Nicaragua, Anastasio Somoza was the President. Somoza had a history of friendship with the United States including the significant act of friendship in 1961 when Somoza, who at that time was head of the military in Nicaragua [and known as the behind-the-scenes leader of the Somoza dynasty after his graduation from West Point] offered President Kennedy the use of Nicaragua as a base for the U.S. incursion into the Bay of Pigs in Cuba. Kennedy used it. Fidel Castro then warned that revenge would be taken on Somoza for helping President Kennedy. Just as significantly as what he did in 1961, Somoza, who had become Vice President of Nicaragua as well as retaining control of the military, was the only leader in Latin America to offer President Johnson and then President Nixon his nation's troops to fight beside U.S. troops in Vietnam. Although neither U.S. President called on him to do it, both Presidents Johnson and Nixon were deeply appreciative. Not President Carter who abandoned Somoza who by this time had become President of Nicaragua, with Carter demanding Somoza leave Nicaragua because of charges of human rights violations. The Sandinistas, who were proxies of the Soviet Union, then came into Nicaragua in full force. Somoza was forced to leave office, going to Miami. President Carter denied him refuge in Miami or anywhere in the United States. Somoza then went to Paraguay where he was assassinated. His remains were allowed to be buried in Miami; his funeral attended by masses of anti-Castro refugees.

The Central American War started with 40 deaths blamed on President Romero's administration of El Salvador, and because of President Carter's abandonment of El Salvador and Nicaragua, it ended with a fall of those two governments that cost over 70,000 deaths of Central Americans fighting against Soviet proxies who had taken advantage of the opportunity given to them.

El Salvador's Humberto Romero and Nicaragua's Anastasio Somoza were not the only foreign leaders who became victims of abandonment from President Carter. A third one was a friend and ally of seven U.S. Presidents: the Shah of Iran. President Carter told the Shah to release all political prisoners. In trust of U.S. Presidents prior to Carter, it was done. The released prisoners formed the domestic nucleus against the Shah. Next, President Carter sent U.S. General Huyser to Iran to tell Iran's generals to abandon the Shah. Back in the United States, major U.S. media joined the crusade against the Shah including the telecasting of segments against him on CBS' *60*

Minutes and the same anti-Shah message appeared in an ABC Special called, *The Politics of Torture.*

The chain of events was effective. On January the 16th of 1979 the Shah and his family left Iran, traveling to Morocco. Fifteen days later, on the first day of February, the Ayatollah [Sayyid Ruhollah Musavi] Khomeini unsurprisingly returned from exile to Teheran. Ten days after that [February the 11th] the army stepped aside for the takeover of Iran's leadership by the Ayatollah Khomeini. President Carter's State Department was in virtual celebration and the U.S. Ambassador to the United Nations, Andrew Young, stated that "Khomeini will be somewhat of a Saint when we get over the panic."

On February the 14th, only three days after Khomeini's takeover, his Revolutionary Guard stormed the U.S. Embassy in Teheran, taking over Ambassador William Sullivan's office and the Embassy surrendered. Ambassador Sullivan's staff was kicked, frisked and searched. The staff members were asked if any were Muslims and those who said "no" were beaten.

The Ayatollah Khomeini ordered the Revolutionary Guard out of the Embassy and the U.S. State Department regarded that as evidence that the takeover of the Embassy was an aberration and that Khomeini was not behind it. That proved to be inaccurate.

It was, instead, a dress rehearsal for what would happen some nine months later [November the 4th of 1979] when the Embassy was taken over again by a much more competent Revolutionary Guard and the hostage crisis of U.S. diplomats began.

To his great credit, President Carter attempted a hostage rescue. Although it failed, that courageous order of his was one of resolve to bring the Americans home.

The hostage crisis continued and lasted 444 days until the inaugural ceremonies of President Reagan with the release of the hostages 33 minutes after the new President said *"So help me God"* in his Oath of Office. Negotiations had been made through Algeria starting within days after President-elect Reagan had won the election in November. [The negotiations included U.S. Deputy Secretary of State Warren Christopher negotiating a deal with Iran during those closing months of the Carter Administration. The term "negotiations" was not used since the world had been told that the United States would not negotiate with terrorists.] The Algerian Government was used as a conduit assuming the role of a third nation middle-source in which the United States agreed to revoke all trade sanctions and withdraw all claims against Iran. The agreement barred and precluded prosecution against Iran of any pending or future claims of the United States or of U.S. nationals rising out of the hostage crisis. Another provision in the agreement was that the United States would freeze all the U.S. assets of the Shah and assets of any close relatives of the Shah, with the United States handing those assets to the Khomeini government of Iran, estimated to be some eight billion dollars. In addition the United States would order all persons within U.S. jurisdiction to report to the U.S. Treasury any information known to them regarding such property and assets, and "the United States pledges that it is, and from now on will be, the policy of the United States not to intervene, directly or indirectly, politically or militarily, in Iran's internal affairs."

It was the Carter Administration's deal that Khomeini could not refuse since there was the fear of the unknown in President Reagan who was about to enter office and might do what had not been done: retaliate with force—although Reagan never made any direct statement regarding that.

The Ayatollah Khomeini, not wanting to give President Carter the prestige of being President when the hostages were freed, waited until those 33 minutes after he left office to release them. President Reagan then immediately and magnanimously appointed President Carter to be his official representative in greeting the returned hostages when they landed in Wiesbaden, Germany from Teheran, Iran.

During the Carter Administration, the Shah and his family did not stay in Morocco as the Moroccan government asked them to leave. That began a succession of arrivals and demands to leave: the Bahamas, then Mexico, then the United States, then Panama, and finally the Shah and his family accepted President Anwar Sadat's invitation to come and stay in Egypt. President Sadat gave him a welcome in Cairo fitting a Chief of State. And that's where the Shah died.

Egypt's President Sadat knew that what he was doing would further endanger his own life by exhibiting such friendship to the Shah and his family. Sadat already had enough domestic opposition and had been the recipient of enough fury by other Arab States by signing a peace agreement with Israel and giving Israel diplomatic relations, unlike any other Arab Government at the time. [Jordan came 15 years later.] Sadat was assassinated in 1981.

The fourth abandonment of President Carter was announced while the U.S. Congress had left D.C. for its Christmas vacation of 1978. President Carter surprisingly requested television prime time on December the 15th to tell the nation that he was giving diplomatic relations to the People's Republic of China. That meant that according to the long-held demands of the government of the People's Republic of China, President Carter agreed to break diplomatic relations with Taiwan; remove all U.S. troops from Taiwan, and abrogate the Mutual Defense Treaty between the U.S. and Taiwan that began in 1954. The government of the People's Republic of China had made that offer of those three stipulations to President Nixon back in 1972 and within one second President Nixon rejected them. President Nixon briefed Vice President Ford on what had happened and when the offer was later given to President Ford, he quickly repeated the refusal of President Nixon. The same stipulations were made of President Carter and, uniquely, he agreed to have diplomatic relations under those conditions demanded by the People's Republic of China.

In all four cases, human rights were not enhanced by President Carter's abandonment of friendly governments. Instead, the unfriendly governments that took over increased human rights violations.

On October the 9th of 1981, the night before the entombment of Egypt's President Sadat, a number of U.S. delegates to the ceremonies were sitting in a room off to the side of the lobby of the Al Ahram Hotel. They were telling stories to one another about the late President Sadat. One prominent U.S. diplomat told the others in that room that he was in Cairo shortly after the Shah's arrival there, and he reminded the others of how the Shah had been forced to leave country after country and that only Anwar Sadat of Egypt would accept the Shah, inviting him and his family to live in Cairo. That diplomat said when he was alone with Sadat, "I told him that it must have been a very difficult decision for him to invite the Shah to come to Cairo, knowing that his invitation might cause him—cause Sadat—some dangerous repercussions. President Sadat was very indignant at the suggestion and he answered me by saying, 'Difficult? Why should it be difficult to decide how to treat a friend? For me there was no difficulty.'"

President Sadat's clear response could have been expected because he was not a neutral. It was the diplomat's statement that exposed his own lack of principle. Sadat's clarity should, in fact, be the permanent policy of the United States. Why should it be difficult to decide how to treat a friend? For the United States there should be no difficulty.

5

ROTATING OBAMA'S GLOBE ACROSS THE ATLANTIC TO EUROPE

THE CZECH REPUBLIC AND POLAND

The first stop was Prague.

Although as President Obama would begin his fourth year in office he would tell the nation that *"the renewal of American leadership can be felt across the globe,"* Prague did not seem to agree with that view.

Nor was there agreement that *"Our oldest alliances in Europe and Asia are stronger than ever."*

During the last year of the Bush Administration, on July the 8th of 2008 while the campaign for the next President was being waged in the United States, President Bush's Secretary of State Condoleezza Rice was in Prague signing an agreement between the United States and the Czech Republic for a long-sought advanced radar system station to be located in the Czech Republic. With Iran as a threat, the radar system's purpose was to be able to track incoming missiles. That radar system was planned in association with an equally long-sought scheduled agreement with Poland for a ground-based missile base to launch ten interceptor missiles from silos after the Czech Republic's warning of incoming missiles, so as to destroy the incoming missiles before hitting their targets. [This agreement with Poland was signed the following month on August the 20th of 2008.] In short, it was a two-nation series of agreements with the United States to guard Europe against incoming missiles, having been formally proposed in early 2007 after several years of consultations with the Czech Republic and Poland.

At the signing in the Czech Republic, Secretary of State Rice said that the United States and its allies and other friends face Iran as "a growing missile threat that is growing ever longer and ever deeper and where the Iranian appetite for nuclear technology to this point is still unchecked."

In reference to whether or not an incoming President of the United States (at the time unknown as to who it would be) would endorse these agreements, Secretary of State Rice said, "It is hard for me to believe that an American President is not going to want to have the capability to defend our territory and the territory of our allies."

Wrong.

The new President was Barack Obama who, in his first year in office [September the 17th, 2009] cancelled the agreements.

One of the great traditions of the United States, and a tradition of many other democracies, was that a new elected leader, other than in the most extraordinary circumstances, would uphold the international agreements made by the predecessors of the new leader. In that way foreign policy agreements of the United States would be considered to be a pact of the nation rather than a temporary agreement subject to change by the next elected leader. [As example, while the Panama Canal Treaties were being debated in the United States, Ronald Reagan made an issue of his opposition to those treaties advocated by President Carter. By the time former Governor Reagan became President, the agreements had been signed and President Reagan declined to do anything to rescind them. The agreements were the word of the United States, not the word of a man.]

Polish Prime Minister Donald Tusk and President of Poland Lech Kaczynski, as well as Czech Republic President Vaclav Klaus had weathered storms of protest while these previously made agreements regarding missile defense had been under discussion with the United States. There were those in their countries who opposed such agreements, and more particularly there was not only opposition from the Russian leadership of Russia's President Dmitri Medvedev and Prime Minister Vladimir Putin but warnings from them, threatening to target Russian missiles on such planned emplacements in both Poland and the Czech Republic. Through all this, the leaders of Poland and the Czech Republic did not give in to the pressures against the agreements, choosing to stick with the United States.

But then came the surprise of a reversal from the United States with President Obama saying that it would be more effective to have *"stronger, smarter and swifter defenses of American forces and America's allies"* by smaller interceptors, first to be deployed on ships at sea with *"technology that is both proven and cost effective"* and perhaps to be put on European soil at a later time.

President of Poland, Lech Kaczynski said that "President Obama's new strategy leaves Poland in a dangerous grey zone between Western Europe and the Old Soviet sphere."

The Polish hero of the Cold War, Lech Walesa, who later became President of Poland said, "I can see what kind of policy the Obama Administration is pursuing toward this part of Europe. The way we are being approached needs to change."

Poland's newspaper, *Fakt*, printed on its front page, "Betrayal! The U.S. sold us to Russia and stabbed us in the back."

The Czech Republic's newspaper *Mlada Fronta Dnes* headlined, "There will not be radar. Russia won."

Another newspaper of the Czech Republic, *Hospodarske Novine* wrote, "An ally we rely on has betrayed us and exchanged us for its own better relations with Russia, of which we are rightly afraid."

A former Prime Minister of the Czech Republic, Mirek Topolanek said, "This is bad news. After 20 years of our path into Europe-Atlantic structures and our very active involvement there, the process is being halted."

There were, however, compliments from Russia's President and Prime Minister. President Dmitri Medvedev said, "We appreciate the responsible approach of the U.S. President towards implementing our agreements. I am ready to continue the dialogue." Prime Minister Vladimir Putin said, "The latest decision by President Obama inspires hope and I do anticipate that this correct and brave decision will be followed by others."

Two and one-half years later, [March the 26th of 2012 in Seoul, South Korea] at a meeting between Presidents Obama and Medvedev, apparently there had been a discussion regarding U.S. missile defense when a live microphone revealed a private conversation between those two Presidents.

President Obama said, *"On all these issues, but particularly missile defense, this can be solved."* Since Medvedev would soon be replaced as President by Vladimir Putin, President Obama added, *"But it's important for him to give me space."*

Medved answered, "I understand. I understand your message about space; space for you."

"This is my last election. After the election I have more flexibility."

"I understand. I will transmit this information to Vladimir. And I stand with you."

Why didn't President Obama transmit this information earlier and currently to Poland's Donald Tusk and Lech Kaczynski and to the Czech Republic's Vaclav Klaus and most importantly, transmit this information earlier and currently to the voters of the United States?

Both the public decision regarding missile defense of 2009 and the revelation made possible by an open microphone of 2012, there was evidence that there was, in effect, a trade: Poland's Donald Tusk and Lech Kaczynski and the Czech Republic's Vaclav Klaus traded for Russia's Dmitri Medvedev and Vladimir Putin. But it is likely they were not the biggest victors of all. Depending on Iran's potential missile capabilities and nuclear development, the biggest victor in all of this could well be the Ayatollah Khamenei.

THE UNITED KINGDOM

The United States has enjoyed *Special Relationships* with a number of nations not by law, but by tradition. The two most prominent of them have been Great Britain and Israel with those *Special Relationships* of the United States known for many decades throughout the world.

During President John F. Kennedy's Administration, the people of the United States, through an Act of Congress signed by the President, gave impetus to that *special relationship* with Great Britain by granting to former Prime Minister of the United Kingdom, Winston Churchill, an Honorary Citizenship of the United States. At that time [April the 9th of 1963] it was the only Honorary Citizenship of the United States granted to anyone. As well as that honorary citizenship, President Kennedy honored Sir Winston Churchill with a replica of a U.S. Passport as an Honorary Citizen's document.

Exactly three years later, during President Lyndon B. Johnson's Administration, [on April the 9th of 1966] Secretary of State Dean Rusk unveiled a statue of the late Winston Churchill standing with his left hand holding his cane and his right hand extended upward holding two fingers in his familiar "V for Victory" symbol that he used throughout World War II. Most significantly, the statue was placed outside the Ambassador's Residence of the British Embassy on D.C.'s Massachusetts Avenue [Embassy Row], with the statue's left foot placed on British territory and his right foot on U.S. territory.

In recognition of his mother being an American citizen [born in Brooklyn, New York], the plaque near the statue says in part: "…One foot stands on United States soil, one on British Embassy grounds, a symbol of Churchill's Anglo-American descent, and of the Alliance he did so much to forge in war and peace."

Shortly after the 9-11, 2001 attacks on the United States, Prime Minister Tony Blair of the United Kingdom arranged for President George W. Bush to receive a bronze bust of former Prime Minister Winston Churchill as a loan from the United Kingdom's Government Art Collection. Above the fireplace in the Oval Office President Bush had a painting of President George Washington; to the left of the fireplace was an end-table holding only a bust of President Abraham Lincoln, and now to the right of the fireplace was a matching end-table holding only that bust of Prime Minister Winston Churchill.

After President Bush won a second term of the Presidency, the loan was extended to him.

Four years later a spokesman for the British Embassy in Washington, D.C. said, "We have made it clear that we would be pleased to extend the loan should Mr. Obama so wish." But no response was received.

It was later revealed that the bust was removed from the Oval Office and placed into storage by White House curators. In a short while the British Embassy spokesman said, "The bust of Sir Winston Churchill by Sir Jacob Epstein was uniquely lent to a foreign head of state, President George W. Bush from the Government Art Collection in the wake of 9/11 as a signal of the strong transatlantic relationship. It was lent for the first term of office of President Bush. When the President was elected for his second and final term, the loan was extended until January 2009. The new President has decided not to continue this loan and the bust has been returned. It is on display at the Ambassador's Residence."

When Prime Minister of the United Kingdom, Gordon Brown came to the White House in March of 2009, he was not granted a formal press conference usually held with the President and leader of a foreign nation, nor was there a formal dinner.

As is the custom for visiting leaders of foreign nations to the White House, the visiting leader gave a gift to the President and the President gave a gift to the visiting leader. The Prime Minister's gift to President Obama was a wooden pen holder that was carved from a long-ago ship that had been used to end the slave trade. President Obama's gift to Prime Minister Brown was a number of DVDs of Hollywood films. It was revealed in London's *Sunday Telegraph* that "they were not compatible with British DVD players." The *Sunday Telegraph* went on to say that "The real views of many in the Obama administration were laid bare by a State Department official involved in planning the Brown visit who reacted with fury when questioned by the *Sunday Telegraph* about why the event was so low-key. The U.S. State Department official dismissed any notion of the special relationship, saying: 'There's nothing special about Britain. You're just the same as the other 190 countries in the world. You shouldn't expect special treatment.'"

The London Evening Standard also reported the story and provided the statement that "a senior state department official retorted, 'There's nothing special about Britain.'"

This was not the end of the President's gifts to the leaders of Great Britain. During his March 31st through April 3rd 2009 trip to Great Britain, President Obama [on April the 1st] gave Queen Elizabeth II a gift. It was an iPod. It was loaded with his 2004 speech at the Democrat's National Convention and his 2009 Inaugural Address as well as photos of the Queen's 2007 visit to the White House and Jamestown, Virginia. There were unconfirmed reports that the Queen already had an iPod which was silver and bought either by or at the suggestion of her second son, Prince Andrew.

Making things worse, at the United Nations General Assembly meeting in September of 2009 attended by both President Obama and Prime Minister Gordon Brown, according to *The London Evening Standard*, "Obama turned down repeated requests from Brown for a meeting."

Two years later, in 2011 the disagreements between the United Kingdom intensified when the United States rose above personal insults from the Obama Administration to a change of U.S. policy that risked rupturing the *Special Relationship* between the United States and the United Kingdom even more severely. What was either not known by President Obama or disregarded by him was the following:

At the beginning of President Reagan's administration if someone came into the State Department with clairvoyance and said that in about a year there would be a new threat of war going on somewhere, the guessing would have been between Israel and Lebanon or between Jordan and Syria or between China and Vietnam or between Nicaragua and Honduras or between the Soviet Union and anywhere. There would easily have been enough places to make a selection. Not likely would there be a foreign policy expert who would have guessed the two parties would be Great Britain and Argentina. But those were the two parties.

The war would be fought over the British Falkland Islands; a cluster of hundreds of very small islands with a total population of less than 2,000 residents at the time, most of them living on the two largest islands of the Falklands. Great Britain had possession of the Falklands since 1833. The islands were located some 300 miles from Argentina's shoreline and some 8,000 miles down the Atlantic Ocean from Great Britain. Argentina wanted them, claimed them, and called them not the Falkland Islands but the Malvinas Islands.

Prior to the Reagan administration, during President Carter's administration, there was the revelation of the potential of oil in the Falklands' territorial waters. Argentina fired on a ship from Great Britain. No casualties; no damage. Both nations recalled their Ambassadors but the two nations retained diplomatic relations. They then cooled down and exchanged Ambassadors again. The dispute didn't end but seemed to be under control. For the United States this was little more than one of many disputes of borders between nations friendly to the United States.

But it became much more than that on April the 2nd of 1982 when Argentina launched an armed invasion of the Falklands.

The residents of the Falklands staunchly supported Great Britain's jurisdiction and despised any Argentine quest to take possession of them. Now came a military dimension to the conflict.

For President Reagan it was a particularly unwanted crisis between those two nations. While the U.S. wanted the support of Latin American states against Soviet proxies in El Salvador and Nicaragua it was obvious that U.S. support of Great Britain against Argentina was sure to enrage the very Latin American states that were wanted as supporters. Even though the State Department strongly advised neutrality, the course of President Reagan was clear in support of Prime Minister Margaret Thatcher's government of Great Britain and his opposition to General Leopoldo Galiteri's government of Argentina.

Both nations could use "the good offices" of the United States for discussions, with the United States hosting negotiations between the two parties in conflict. Many of the President's advisors and the State Department endorsed the hosting of the United States. However, President Reagan had already made up his mind on U.S. policy: rescind the offer of the "good offices" unless Prime Minister Thatcher wanted those offices retained.

Since March the 31st, two days before the Argentine invasion of the Falklands, the Soviet Union had launched at least eight satellites into orbit over the South Atlantic. It was apparent that the information received by the Soviets tracking of the British Fleet toward the Falklands was being shared with the Galiteri government of Argentina.

President Reagan said he would like to see the Soviet Union "butt out." In addition, Secretary of State Al Haig who had originally been an advocate of negotiations, said that "at the outset of the crisis, blandishments already were being offered by both Cuba and the Soviet Union." Castro's Vice President said, "Cuba recognizes Argentina's sovereignty over the islands and supports Argentina's people in its desire to regain the control of the islands."

Great Britain now had close to two-thirds of its navy heading toward the Falklands and Great Britain's Prince Andrew was en route aboard a carrier where he was assigned as a helicopter pilot.

The United States was giving both overt and covert support to Great Britain including detailed intelligence information going to the British on Argentina's armed forces, and the U.S. was supporting Great Britain's threat to sink any Argentine ship approaching the Falkland Islands.

Beyond all that was the long-term *Special Relationship* between the United States and the United Kingdom: When the United States had imposed a grain embargo on the Soviet Union because of its invasion of Afghanistan, Great Britain immediately announced willingness to join the embargo while Argentina refused to participate. Great Britain had more recently supported U.S. sanctions against the Soviet Union because of the imposition of martial law in Poland while major European states looked the other way, claiming the order of martial law was an internal matter for Poland.

U.K. Ambassador to the United States, Sir Nicholas Henderson explained the crisis of the Falklands clearly when he compared it to the recent American hostage crisis in Iran: "British citizens who live in the Falkland Islands are being held hostage by Argentina. These are British citizens who do not want to be under the jurisdiction of Argentina."

Seventy-four days and 907 lives after Argentina's invasion of the Falklands, the war was over with the total withdrawal of the Argentine military from the Falklands in an overwhelming victory for Great Britain.

By President Reagan's support of Great Britain, he lost the support of many nations in the Organization of American States as he knew was bound to happen. But President Reagan concluded that the course Prime Minister Thatcher had chosen was the right course for Great Britain, for the people of the Falklands, and the right course for the United States. The *Special Relationship* was securely intact. At least for 29 years.

In 2011 the Obama Administration embarked on undoing what the Reagan support of Great Britain had accomplished. The following are excerpts from the questions and answers of the February 25th, 2011 U.S State Department Daily Press Briefing of Assistant Secretary of State for Public Affairs, P.J. Crowley and members of the press:

Q. Yesterday, you were asked about the Argentine written dispute on the Falklands, and you said you were neutral on the question of sovereignty. Can I ask why you're neutral on the question of sovereignty? If you recognize the UK administration, why are you neutral on sovereignty?

A. Well, I mean to the extent that there is a dispute between Britain and Argentina over the status of the islands—whatever you want to call them—we believe that that should be handled through dialogue.

Q. But why are you neutral on it and why do you say whatever you want to call them (inaudible)?

A. We—I mean, our position on neutrality on the competing claims over sovereignty is a longstanding United States position.

Q. On the Falklands? On this specific instance?

A. Or the Malvinas, depending on how you see it.

Q. So you're willing to accept the possibility that they should be called the Malvinas and they should be Argentine?

A. Well, no, we remain neutral, which means we support resumption of negotiations between Argentina and the United Kingdom to find a peaceful solution. We think this can and should be handled through normal diplomatic channels, and we support dialogue.

On March 1st of 2011, four days after that press conference, against the wishes of the United Kingdom, Secretary of State Hillary Clinton met with Argentine President Cristina Fernandez de Kirchner and discussed the dispute between the United Kingdom and Argentina over the Falklands. Secretary Clinton stated that the United States was neutral on the issue of sovereignty.

Although the statement reflected the policy of President Obama, he didn't personally make a public statement about the Falklands until some 13 months later on April the 15th of 2012. At a Summit of the Americas news conference in Cartagena, Colombia he was asked about the issue and he answered, *"In terms of the Maldives or the Falklands, whatever your preferred term,"* [he meant to say "the Malvinas or the Falklands" since the Maldives Islands were southwest of India in the Indian Ocean, over 1800 miles away from the islands being addressed] *"our position on this is that we are going to remain neutral. We have good relations with both Argentina and Great Britain, and we are looking forward to them being able to continue to dialogue on this issue. But this is not something we typically intervene in."*

Of course we typically do. Maybe he didn't know that the United States had been *typically* involved in totality on the side of Great Britain's jurisdiction over the Falklands before he came into office.

To be alive and witness events and then assume a position of neutrality is nothing better than to choose not to exist at all at a time of conflict for others.

6

THE MEDITERRANEAN AND MIDDLE EAST THEATER

TUNISIA

Although it would become known as the Arab Spring of 2011, it was not spring nor 2011 when it started. It all started a few days before winter began in 2010.

Tunisia's President [Zine El Abadine] Ben-Ali, who for 23 years ran one of the most secular Arab states, was continuing his support of the United States in its war against Radical Islamists. The United States trained Ben-Ali's military in the U.S., and Ben-Ali's government participated in the Trans-Sahara Counter-Terrorism Partnership. Domestically, Ben-Ali led decades of privatization from those things that had been owned by the state, but his nation was now going through an economic crisis with food shortages, low employment and high inflation with all signs indicating that the worth of the Tunisian dinar would continue its decline.

It was Monday, December the 17th when 26 year old Mohamed Bouazizi, a seller of vegetables from a street-cart, committed the act of setting himself on fire in the streets of Sidi Bouzid in Tunisia. According to reports from residents of that city, a policewoman told him to stop selling his vegetables without a license. He didn't move and she yelled at him and spat at him, and she had his vegetable cart taken away. The reports went on to give the account that he was selling produce from an unlicensed cart because he had to support his brothers and sisters and could not find a job under the severe economic conditions of Tunisia.

He was brought to a hospital. The fire from the self-immolation, as terrible as it was, had effect on even more than Mohamed Bouazizi, as it caused the spark that set the nation into a revolution. On January the 3rd of 2011 there were massive street demonstrations against the government; the protesters demonstrating against unemployment and other economic hardships. Within days demonstrations became country-wide including protestors going through the streets of the capital city of Tunis. President Ben-Ali visited the young man at the hospital to express his concern. The next day, Mohamed Bouazizi died.

The Secretary General of Hezbollah, General Hassan Nasrallah complimented the demonstrators in Tunisia. So did President Obama who said on Friday, January the 14th, "I have no doubt that Tunisia's future will be brighter if it is guided by the voices of the Tunisian people." That was the day when President Ben-Ali was ousted, fleeing with his wife, Leila, and three children to Jeddah, Saudi Arabia. His government was done.

Months later, on October the 23rd of 2011, Tunisia held an election for its Constituent Assembly. The Islamist En-Nahda [Renaissance Party] won a plurality of 41%, giving it 90 seats in the 217 seat Assembly. Along with minority parties, the parliament became dominated by Islamists.

Throughout the preceding demonstrations, east of Tunisia there had been an audience watching what was happening in that country. The viewers were in the most important Arab state in the world: Egypt.

Through cyberspace above the Mediterranean, through the Internet, through Dailymotion, through Twitter, through Facebook, through YouTube, and through other electronic communications, Egyptians saw and heard the news of the success of demonstrators in Tunisia ousting their President Ben-Ali.

EGYPT

On Sunday, January the 23rd of 2011, the Egyptian sunrise exhibited demonstrators in Cairo's Tahrir Square. Armed with all kinds of electronic devices, those in the square were continuing to keep up with events in Tunisia and were now demanding similar events come to Egypt, including the ouster of Egypt's President Hosni Mubarak. The demonstrations became massive two days later, on January the 25th.

That night President Obama gave his State of the Union Address [January the 25th of 2011]. In that speech he said that Americans saw the *"desire to be free in Tunisia, where the will of the people proved more powerful than the writ of a dictator. And tonight, let us be clear: The United States of America stands with the people of Tunisia, and supports the democratic aspirations of all people."*

Who would be leading Tunisia after Ben-Ali was unknown by President Obama; was unknown by those applauding; was unknown by anyone. The day after President Obama's State of the Union Address, on January the 26th, Tunisian arrest warrants were issued for Ben-Ali, his wife, other members of his family, and former ministers of his government.

Now the world gave attention to what they called the Arab Spring. Cairo's Tahrir Square was filled with protestors and much of the world including many in the United States were cheering in support of them in their demand for President Mubarak to leave office.

Hosni Mubarak had become President after serving as Anwar Sadat's Vice President. On October the 6th of 1981 President Sadat was on a reviewing stand watching a military parade in front of a large crowd. President Sadat, Vice President Mubarak and most of the others at the event were looking upwards at Mirage jets flying in exhibition when a troop-truck in the parade stopped in front of the reviewing stand and six uniformed men later found to be members of Jama'at al Jihad known as the Islamic Jihad, an offshoot of the Muslim Brotherhood, ran to the reviewing stand, opening fire. President Sadat was killed and Vice President Mubarak was wounded.

From that day forward Hosni Mubarak was President of Egypt, maintaining the peace treaty with Israel that had been achieved by Anwar Sadat. As the years went by he proved to be a staunch ally of the United States in the War against Radical Islamists. Mubarak's emphasis was in closing tunnels from the use of Hamas on the border between Gaza and Egypt. Moreover, he supported President George W. Bush's actions against Saddam Hussein's government of Iraq, and gave quick diplomatic relations to Iraq's new Post-Saddam government.

No responsible U.S. President would have welcomed the risk of someone unknown to follow Mubarak, particularly while the United States was in a war in which President Mubarak was an ally. There is, instead, ample evidence that FDR, Truman, Eisenhower, Kennedy, Johnson, Nixon, Ford, Reagan, Bush (41), Clinton and Bush (43) would have supported President Mubarak during the Cairo demonstrations of 2011 in Tahrir Square.

There was the issue of loyalty and an issue common to those Presidents in having to make a choice between supporting undemocratic leaders who supported the United States or allowing them to fall with threatening consequences. The epitome of such decision-making was FDR and Churchill during World War II who had as a chief ally, of all people, Joseph Stalin of the Soviet Union. There is no doubt that Joseph Stalin was outrageously evil, but Adolph Hitler was also outrageously evil, and *at the time* Hitler was the greater immediate danger.

The question regarding the Egyptian demonstrators can surely be asked, "But wouldn't the U.S. want democracy for those who demonstrated in Tahrir Square?" Of course. World liberty is the ultimate objective of the United States as so adamantly expressed particularly in major speeches of Presidents John F. Kennedy and George W. Bush. But during *a time of war* the first objective must be to win or the ultimate objective of world liberty would automatically be placed beyond future reach. The protestors demanded a leader get out but did not say who they wanted in. Most likely the majority didn't know who they wanted to lead their nation.

At the outset, the protestors in Tahrir Square continually talked to interviewers from the world's media about low wages, rising prices and increasing unemployment. They had the same major complaints of those who were demonstrating in the *democracies* of Europe: Greece, Portugal, Spain, Ireland, Italy, and the UK where those in massive protest at the time had similar complaints against weak economies and their government's austerity programs. It is likely that even if Egypt was democratic while the economy was struggling, and having watched Tunisia, they would have had the demonstrations they staged in Tahrir Square. It was difficult to believe that the demonstrations came only from some spontaneous quest for *democracy* after some five thousand years of *non*-democracy.

Undoubtedly there were those who truly did want a democracy, inspired by events in Tunisia, but it was the stress on economics that dominated the complaints of the early demonstrations. When Tahrir Square became more and more central in world-wide news events, the advocacy of the demonstrators in the Square changed from economics to democracy.

It was reminiscent of the Los Angeles, California protests supporting illegal immigrants in 2006 in televised massive marches waving flags of Mexico. Even defenders of those demonstrators called such visual representations as thoughtless and warned they were defeating their very purpose by waving Mexican flags. In short, if they advocated living in the United States why were they waving flags of Mexico? That was no way to influence Americans. The criticism was heard by the leaders of the protests and the next demonstration took place by masses waving flags of the United States. Similarly, after the first few days of televised interviews with demonstrators in Cairo's Tahrir Square, the earlier complaints were changed. They came to realize that demanding democracy was so much better received than those earlier complaints about the economy.

All this was viewed by the Muslim Brotherhood who very carefully took advantage of the circumstances, not admitting their involvement in the events, and to satisfy the skeptics, they also stated they didn't want to enter the process of potential future elections.

Secretary General of Hezbollah General Hassan Nasrallah praised Egyptian demonstrators for "pushing out a regime that has maintained peace with Israel."

On February the 11th, President Mubarak, under severe pressure to leave office, resigned from the presidency and left Cairo to go to his residence in the southeast city of the Sinai; Sharm el-Shiekh. This was followed by orders to Mubarak not to leave Egypt as he was placed under house arrest on February the 28th.

The crime for which he was charged was the suspicion that he ordered his troops to kill many protestors during the demonstrations against his government. Although never to be written in their texts, it was much more likely he was being held for maintaining the designation of illegality of the Muslim Brotherhood during his years in office, and for maintaining diplomatic relations with Israel throughout his administration.

Two months later on April the 12th former President Mubarak was stricken with a heart attack and entered a hospital in Sharm el-Sheik. The following day Mubarak's two sons, Alaa and Gamal, were imprisoned.

In 42 days [May the 24th] Mubarak was ordered to stand

trial, and the order was accompanied with the announcement that he could face the death penalty. It should be expected that after learning the condition of former President Mubarak in Sharm el Sheikh, the United States would, at a minimum, publically express concern. If nothing else, it would have been a statement to the world that at least the United States cared. But that message was not sent. Even among many Americans, that message was not expected. Unfortunately in the new morality, loyalty to a friend was not an issue; it was considered to be an intrusion.

Almost simultaneous with all this, Mohammed Badie from the Muslim Brotherhood announced that a political party of the Muslim Brotherhood had been formed with the name of the "Freedom and Justice Party." The previous claim of not having any ambition to enter the political process was now annulled by its new name. Those who had supported the Muslim Brotherhood immediately tried to calm nerves by saying that the Muslim Brotherhood had support from only 20 to 30% of the people, making participation in the electoral process irrelevant.

In a domestic sense the change of name could be thought to be officially ending its over six decades of illegality and overriding the 2007 constitutional amendment prohibiting any political party from being centered on a religion. In a global sense it sounded like it had moral goals: freedom and justice. But its goals were more likely neither freedom nor justice but rather the same goals it had when it carried the name of the Muslim Brotherhood.

On August the 3rd of 2011, near Cairo, former President Mubarak was brought into a court room on a gurney and put into a cage with his two sons and Egypt's former Interior Minister; all four wearing white prisoner's clothing.

When the world thought that would end the demonstrations, surprisingly for many, there were still protests every Friday in Tahrir Square. The demonstrators were now rejecting the transitional government, and wanted quicker economic changes and quicker punishment for former President Mubarak whose continuing trial dates had been rescheduled.

Attention had now turned to the Coptic Christians, the largest Christian community in the Middle East. Previously protected by Mubarak, now their churches were being burned down. When Christians protested and attempted a Cairo downtown sit-in, they were attacked. The Associated Press reported that "a speeding military vehicle jumped up onto a sidewalk and rammed into some of the Christians."

President Obama's Press Secretary, Jay Carney, said, "The President is deeply concerned about the violence in Egypt that has led to a tragic loss of life among demonstrators and security forces. The United States expresses our condolences to the families and loved ones of all who were killed or injured, and stands with the Egyptian people in this painful and difficult time. Now is a time for restraint on all sides so that Egyptians can move forward together to forge a strong and united Egypt. As the Egyptian people shape their future, the United States continues to believe that the rights of minorities—including Copts—must be respected, and that all people have the universal rights of peaceful protest and religious freedom. We also note Prime Minister Sharaf's call for an investigation and appeal to all parties to refrain from violence. These tragic events should not stand in the way of timely elections and a continued transition to democracy that is peaceful, just and inclusive."

Note that within the statement, as sympathetic as it was, there was the call for "restraint on *all sides*" and reference to *"all parties* to refrain from violence." That is straight from the book of State Department diplomacy in making moral equivalence of two parties in conflict. But there is no moral equivalence in this. The Coptic Christians and their supporters had every right and moral necessity to fight against those who were killing them.

Between the second and the third and final rounds of voting for members of Egypt's People's Assembly, on January the 5th of 2012 at the U.S. State Department Daily Press Briefing held by Press Spokeswoman Victoria Nuland there were questions on whether or not the Muslim Brotherhood would abide by President Sadat's signature on the Peace Treaty with Israel that had been upheld by President Mubarak. The questions were between members of the press with the answers by the State Department's Victoria Nuland:

Q. Okay. We have the deputy head of the Muslim Brotherhood in an interview with Al Hayat saying that they don't regard the peace treaty with Israel as binding, that they didn't sign it, and if they come to power, they might put it to a referendum. Do you have any reaction to that? Are you—is this something that you're trying to seek more clarification on from them?

A. Well, we've seen this press report. I would say that it is one member of the MB. We have had other assurances from the party with regard to their commitment not only to universal human rights, but to the international obligations that the Government of Egypt has undertaken. As we've said again and again, not only with regard to Egypt but with regard to other states in that region in transition, we expect that legitimate parties will not only support universal human rights, but will also (inaudible) continue to support international obligations made by their governments.

Q. So as far as you understand, this isn't officially the Muslim Brotherhood position that was reflected in that interview? You still think that they are bound to uphold the treaty?

A. We—they have made commitments to us along those regards, and as I said, we will judge these parties by what they do.

[There were then questions on another subject and then the following on the trial of President Mubarak, followed by a continuation of the subject of the Peace Treaty.]

Q. As you've no doubt seen that the prosecutor in the trial of former President Mubarak has said that they're seeking the death penalty, and I'm just wondering if you have any comment on that. Do you think that's an appropriate punishment to be looking for in this case?

A. Not going to comment specifically on that issue. I think you know where we have been, that we want to see this judicial proceeding and any judicial proceedings go forward in conformity with Egyptian law and with international jurisprudence standards.

Q. Victoria, a follow-up on Andy's question on the Muslim Brotherhood. Now, they gave you these assurances in casual conversations, or are they stated policy—the party policy line, or how did they give you their assurances to abide by internationally agreed—(interrupted)

A. Well, let me say that among the reasons that we are trying to meet with different political actors in Egypt, including with the Muslim Brotherhood, is that this isn't a monolithic organization. None of these groups are monolithic. We want to make sure that we have an open dialogue where we are being clear publicly, but we're also being clear privately about our hopes and expectations for Egypt's future, our hopes and expectations that any political actors will respect human rights and will uphold the international obligations of the Egyptian Government. So we have, in that context, had some good reassurances from different interlocutors, and we will continue to seek those kinds of reassurances going forward. Let's go to Iran in the –

Q. I just want to go back to your answer on the Mubarak question.

A. Yeah.

Q. You said you want to see this judicial proceeding as well as any other judicial proceeding go forward in accordance with—what's your—with dot, dot, dot. What's your opinion of the Egyptian judicial system at the moment? Is it capable of meeting these standards?

A. Well, I think the international community is looking to Egypt to set a high standard with this trial and with other procedures going forward now.

Q. But—yeah, but right now do you have confidence—

A. I'm not going to give them a report card, Matt.

Q. Well, in general, what's your feeling about the Egyptian judicial system? Is it capable of delivering a just and fair and—verdict?

A. It is our expectation that they will meet international standards, and that's what we'll be looking for.

After all three rounds of the voting for the People's Assembly were completed [on January the 11th of 2012 and given in final count publicly on February 25, 2012], the results revealed that the highest amount of votes went to the Muslim Brotherhood's Freedom and Justice Party. Second highest was the Salafist Nour Party which was considered to be an equal or more radical group than the Muslim Brotherhood in its demand of Sharia law. Along with other Islamists from some of the smaller parties, it meant that approximately 75% of the entire Egyptian legislature had been won by Islamists. Even before the final count was officially announced, Mohammed Saad al-Katami, a member of the Muslim Brotherhood, was elected as Speaker of the People's Assembly. [January the 23rd of 2012]

Within less than a month, [February the 6th,] the interim government led by the Supreme Council of Armed Forces, Defense Minister Field Marshal Mohammed Hussein Tantawi, refused to let 43 workers [most of whom were foreigners] out of the country with warnings of trials to come, having been charged with "banned activity." Among the 43 were Americans from the International Center for Journalists, the International Republican Institute and the National Democratic Institute, all Non-Governmental Organizations [NGO's] to encourage and assist the institutions of democracy and evaluate U.S. aid. Those organizations had been serving in Egypt during the Mubarak Presidency without political interference. According to the State Department seven Americans quickly sought and received refuge in the U.S. Embassy. In the end [24 days later, on March the 1st] the U.S. Non-Governmental Organizations were required to pay $300,000 bail for each of the seven Americans to be released from travel restrictions while awaiting trial, meaning $2,100,000 in total "ransom." According to the State Department it would be up to each of the Americans to decide if they would return to Egypt for trial.

At the time of the fall of Mubarak, there were those in the world who compared it to the fall of the Berlin Wall. It was a bizarre comparison. The 1989 fall of the Berlin Wall was not accomplished to achieve the end of a man, but to achieve the end of the Soviet Union and the winning of the Cold War. The celebration of Mubarak's fall was much more reminiscent of 1979's fall of the Shah of Iran and the welcome of the Ayatollah Khomeini.

YEMEN

In 1990, after some two decades of war between what had become commonly known as North and South Yemen, Ali Abdallah Saleh became President of a united (at least in name) single nation called the Republic of Yemen.

Yemen was a hotbed for Radical Islamists and received world-wide attention when on October the 12th of 2000, the U.S. Navy's destroyer, the U.S.S. Cole was blasted by members of al-Qaeda while in the port of Aden, killing 17 members of the U.S. Navy. al-Qaeda had already been responsible for a succession of other terrorist attacks, utilizing recruits from all over the world. With their now successful attack on the U.S.S. Cole and later with the prominence of their new leader, Anwar Al-Awlaki, an American citizen by birth, the group became the likely successor to Afghanistan in taking the lead of al-Qaeda. In 2009 the group of jihadists gave themselves the name of al-Qaeda in the Arabian Peninsula known quickly throughout the world as A.Q.A.P. That gave global definition to President Saleh's enemy and it was well known that Saleh, who had been cautious to a fault in earlier years, had now become heavily partnered with the United States in ridding the country of the A.Q.A.P. But then came what was called the Arab Spring bringing about the January 2011 fall of the government of Tunisia, the February fall of the government of Egypt, and the Yemeni Calendar starting in 2011:

JANUARY: Protests of thousands of Yemenis were swarming onto streets with chants of insistence that President Saleh be removed from office.

FEBRUARY: A "Day of Rage" was called for February the 3rd. The day before the scheduled protests, in the hope of heading off demonstrations of any size, President Saleh announced he would leave office in 2013 and stated there would be "no inheritance" of the office being passed on to his son. The pledge didn't work in quelling the demonstrators. Some 20,000 of them formed in Yemen's capital city of Sana'a and marched near Sana'a University.

MARCH: During the last days of March, U.S. administration officials, without attribution, let it be known to selected members of the press that they believed President Saleh should leave office. [Generally when U.S. administration officials say that something is their own belief they are launching a trial balloon for the President, giving the President room to change the decision based on public and media reaction to the "personal" beliefs of officials.] There was little if any public opposition to the official's statements that Saleh should depart the presidency.

APRIL: On April the 12th the protests exceeded any of those in February with a new Sana'a demonstration being the largest ever seen in Yemen, with other demonstrations continuing through the next three days.

MAY: The previously drafted document of the Cooperation Council for the Arab States of the Gulf, known as the Gulf Cooperation Council, became official in calling for President Saleh to leave office and turn the presidency over to his Vice President. In exchange the document stated that President Saleh would receive immunity from prosecution.

JUNE: On June the 3rd a Yemeni protest against President Saleh attacked his Presidential Compound using rocket fire that blasted the mosque within the compound, killing 16 people and wounding some 100 others including President Saleh. The President received multiple shrapnel wounds and burns over 40% of his body. A government aircraft took the President and others to Saudi Arabia for treatment at a Riyadh hospital. Simultaneous with all this, two cities of Yemen fell to the A.Q.A.P. including the capital of Abyan Province, the city of Zanjibar.

JULY: On July the 11th President Saleh was visited at the Riyadh hospital by an envoy from President Obama: John Brennan, the President's Counter-Terrorism advisor. Brennan expressed President Obama's desire for President Saleh to leave office and, as called for by the Gulf Cooperation Council, to surrender his office to his Vice President.

AUGUST: After surgery and some recuperation, on August the 6th President Saleh left Saudi Arabia to return to Yemen, agreeing to leave office and pass the Presidency to the Vice President within ninety days after the agreement called for by the Gulf Cooperation Council would be signed. Likely without coincidence, this was done exactly as had been communicated by President Obama's envoy, John Brennan.

SEPTEMBER: On September the 30th Anwar Al-Awlaki, the leader of A.Q.A.P. was killed by a strike of a U.S. drone. President Obama said, *"He has met his demise because the government and the people of Yemen have joined with the international community in a common effort against al-Qaeda."* What he didn't add was that the government of Yemen that he just complimented, was led by President Saleh who President Obama, through his emissary, had told to leave office.

OCTOBER: On October the 21st of 2011, the United Nations Security Council passed Resolution 2014 calling for an orderly transfer of power in Yemen. As expected, there was no veto or abstention from the United States. It was official that the United States wanted President Saleh out.

NOVEMBER: On November the 23rd President Saleh signed the Gulf Cooperation Council Agreement and U.S. Secretary of State Hillary Clinton said, "The United States applauds the Yemeni Government and the opposition for agreeing to a peaceful and orderly transition of power that is responsive to the aspirations of the Yemeni people . . . We look forward to strengthening our partnership with the Yemeni people and their new government as they address their political, economic, humanitarian, and security challenges."

During this month, al-Qaeda in the Arabian Peninsula (A.Q.A.P.) changed its name to Ansar al-Sharia. The guessing at the State Department was that the organization now wanted to be considered to be separate and apart from al-Qaeda. [It was an example of the expertise of the State Department in being able to offer profound analysis.]

DECEMBER: President Saleh of Yemen made a request to come to the United States for medical treatment. After a conflict of whether or not the U.S. government approved or disapproved, the State Department at first responded that no decision had been reached. Senior officials in Yemen said that the American Embassy already said the visa had been approved while the State Department denied it, then changed their denial into a "no comment."

* * *

In the first month of the new year [January the 22nd of 2012] President Saleh left Yemen, and after spending some days in Oman, landed in the United States [January the 28th] with the understanding that his stay would only be long enough for his medical treatment, which Saleh obeyed and returned home after the treatment.

On February the 25th of 2012, President Saleh was officially out of office and Vice President Abed Rabbu Mansour Hadi took the oath as the new President of Yemen.

Within hours there was a suicide car bombing in Yemen in which 26 people were killed. Taking responsibility was Ansar al-Sharia, better known by its former title of al-Qaeda in the Arabian Peninsula or A.Q.A.P. That was followed by the shooting and killing of Joel Shrum, an American teacher, on March the 18th with Ansar al Sharia's spokesman saying, "The United States, its infidel subjects and interests, are legitimate targets for our jihad." Ansar al-Sharia said the murdered teacher's crime was that he was proselytizing Christianity.

The world acclaim of what was called the Arab Spring was hard to reconcile with other world events. It all began in reaction to the self-immolation of a man in Tunisia while no commensurate world attention was expressed to the more than 35 Tibetans who burned themselves to death in an effort to protest human rights violations taken against Buddhists by the Hu Jintao government of the People's Republic of China. Those self-immolations of Tibetan Buddhists took place between March the 1st of 2009 and May the 2nd of 2012 while greeted without international cries for the unelected Hu Jintao to step down, nor was there any public condemnation of Hu Jintao by U.S. President Obama.

7

THE AXIS POWERS
OF IRAN AND SYRIA

IRAN

During his campaign for the presidency, Senator Barack Obama said: *"Strong countries and strong presidents talk to their adversaries ... I mean think about it; Iran, Cuba, Venezuela—these countries are tiny compared to the Soviet Union. They don't pose a threat to the way the Soviet Union posed a threat to us ... If Iran ever tried to pose a threat to us, they wouldn't stand a chance. And we should use that position of strength that we have, to be bold enough to go ahead and listen. That doesn't mean we agree with them on everything. We might not compromise on any issues, but at least we should find out other areas of potential common interest, and we can reduce some of the tensions that has caused us so many problems around the world."* [May the 18th of 2008.]

During the next year; the first year of his presidency, the placards and shouts of demonstrators in Teheran were: *"Obama! Obama! Either You're with Them—or You're with Us!"* [November the 4th of 2009.]

It was the 30th National Holiday of the takeover of the U.S. Embassy and the demonstrators, at risk of their lives, shouted in opposition to the Iranian government.

It was not only the National Holiday but it was the fifth month of demonstrations of Iranians [that started on June the 13th] after their nation's election results had been announced. Some two million protestors against the government had assembled in Teheran claiming the announced election results were fraudulent. Iranians outside of Teheran agreed with the Teheran demonstrators, and quickly organized protests in other cities, subject to many demonstrators being beaten, imprisoned, and some known to have been killed.

What started all this was an election for the President of Iran with the major competitors for the office being the incumbent, Mahmoud Ahmadinejad and the presidential aspirant, Mir-Hossain Mousavi. The winner of the election was announced to be the re-election of President Ahmadinejad. Most, if not all, demonstrators were not simply protesting the announced results of the election, but by their actions the demonstrators were pro-testing something much larger: the government of the Supreme Leader; the Grand Ayatollah [Sayyid Ali-Hoseyni] Khamenei. They knew the President was an elected mouthpiece for the unelected Ayatollah Khamenei who became the second Supreme Leader since the 1989 death of the Ayatollah Khomeini. [Sorry for the similarity of names but there is nothing we can do about it.]

The President of Iran under the Revolutionary Govern-ment is a position that is not exactly what people of the world think of a presidency. He is more commensurate with the U.S. White House Press Secretary who, in the case of Iran's government, cannot vary beyond a fragile line from what the Grand Ayatollah wants him to say or do. Iran's unelected government runs the show. [Within the government structure, there is the unelected Expediency Council that can veto actions of the elected Parliament. Above the unelected Expediency Council is the unelected Council of Guardians that can disqualify candidates running for office, and has disqualified over 400 candidates in a single election process for the Parliament. Above the unelected Council of Guardians is the unelected Council of Experts of 83 Mullahs, although the number has varied, who, in the case of the death or disability of the Grand Ayatollah, decide who will become the new Grand Ayatollah. Above all those government entities is the Grand Ayatollah himself who is the final authority and spiritual leader of Iran.] Getting rid of Ahmadinejad's presidency alone would not at all mean "regime change."

The demonstrations that started on June the 13th were the largest held in Iran since the Iranian Revolution of 1979. These demonstrators who opposed the government of their country looked toward the United States for moral support. The day passed without a statement. The next day passed without a statement.

On the 15th, in the early evening President Obama said, *"I have always felt, as odious as I feel some of President Ahmadinejad's statements, as deep as the differences that exist between the United States and Iran on core issues, the use of tough hard headed diplomacy; diplomacy without illusions is critical when it comes to pursuing a core set of national security interests."* He then said,

"We will continue to pursue a tough direct dialogue between our two countries."

On the seventh day [June the 20th] a horror was witnessed throughout the world through the internet and television. It was the death of Neda Agha-Soltan, a 26 year old Iranian woman—and it was videotaped by bystanders. She was killed by a bullet shot into her chest during a demonstration of protest. The most frequently distributed video on the internet showed her lying on her back on the road, steps away from the sidewalk as blood spilled from her mouth, nose and chest, with her eyes open.

Her sister, Noda, wrote that Neda "used to say, as we all do and know, that there's a dead depressing air all over Iran. It's everywhere. It's in people's hearts. We are condemned to depression. We are condemned to living without being able to breathe . . . Neda always said she would leave Iran if she had only one day left of her life."

Three days later, on June the 23rd President Obama said, *"It's heartbreaking. It's heartbreaking. And I think that anybody who sees it knows that there's something fundamentally unjust about that."*

Who couldn't make that statement? But President Obama was expected not to be an *observer*, but the *leader* of the free world. Would the United States do nothing about this other than to have its President be heartbroken, pledging to continue the pursuit of a dialogue with the Iranian government?

Despite an estimated two million protestors in the streets of Tehran, it took ten days for President Obama to make strong statements in defense of them.

Too late.

The protestors had been abandoned.

* * *

Beyond its domestic violations of human rights, the government of Iran was becoming more and more of an international threat with its Sejjil-3 Medium Range Ballistic Missiles having a range able to strike U.S. military bases in the Persian Gulf as well as Israel and Sunni Arab states in the region, and some portions of Europe. Although not confirmed, there was the claim that its missile designated the BM-25 could hit targets within larger areas of Europe. There was credible evidence that an Intercontinental Ballistic Missile (ICBM) that could hit the United States from Iran was under development and assisted by the People's Republic of China with their three-stage Dong Feng-31 mobile missile.

There was another potential delivery system: President Mubarak of Egypt did not allow the ships of Iran's government to go through the Suez Canal, but that had changed since Mubarak was overthrown. The Egyptian transitional government rescinded his policy by allowing Iranian ships to pass through the Suez Canal. If Iran should use it to go to the Mediterranean and then all the way to the North Atlantic, even without an ICBM, Iran would have a reasonable route from which to target the United States by currently tested solid fuel missiles launched at sea. Venezuela could also be used as a base for both solid fuel and liquid fueled missiles. None of that can be disregarded.

It is most likely that the ultimate objective of Iran's government was to have nuclear warheads of size, weight, and configuration to be fitted as the payload under the nosecones of ballistic missiles. With some 40 nuclear facilities including their chief site in Isfahan, their nuclear reactor in Bushehr, and their once-secret uranium enrichment plant underground near Qum [known as the Fordow plant] revealed in 2010, it was difficult to believe their claims that their facilities were only developed for energy use alone, particularly with their restrictions on international inspections.

Nevertheless, President Obama said [within an interview conducted by NBC's Matt Lauer recorded on February the 5th of 2012], *"My goal is to resolve this diplomatically, mainly because the only way over the long term we can assure Iran doesn't get a nuclear weapon is by getting them to understand it's not in their interest."*

But it is in their interest.

The *"them"* to which President Obama referred had as their greatest interest the possession of nuclear weapons and joining the world's nuclear club of nine. With that entrance into the club, beyond the potential ability of the Iranian government to launch nuclear weapons was what Iran could do even *prior* to deciding to launch by invoking nuclear blackmail against nations (including against the United States). Iran was correct in assuming that possession alone, without a launch, gives a nation immense international advantages.

It should be noted that while the U.S. government has insisted on "constructive engagement" that has not worked, any number of leaders of Arab Gulf States and some other Arab States have made it quietly known they want military action taken against Iran prior to Iran having nuclear weapon capability. Since 2010 the United States and Israel could have had an alliance with some Sunni Arab nations maintaining silence or a public plausible deniability if some of those states would choose a non-public posture.

From 1979 forward, Iran's government has declared war on the United States, not in a formal written document but in total violations of international law by seizing a foreign embassy and holding American diplomats as prisoners. A foreign embassy is considered part of the foreign government itself and not part of the host country.

Among other declarations of war by Iran, a plan for one was uncovered in 2011 with the plot of the Iranian government to assassinate Adel al-Jubeir, Saudi Arabia's Ambassador to the United States. The idea was to bomb a restaurant in Washington, D.C. where the Ambassador frequently had lunch. Since it would probably be crowded at that time [generally including members of the U.S. Congress and administration appointees] the ones hired by Iran to kill the Ambassador were told that if others in the restaurant were killed it would be "no big deal." The ones hired for the assassination were also supposed to bomb the Embassy of the Kingdom of Saudi Arabia in the Foggy Bottom area of Washington, D.C. near the John F. Kennedy Center for the Performing Arts, the Watergate and Potomac Plaza. The third target was the Embassy of Israel near the University of the District of Columbia. The plot was uncovered by the FBI before the crimes were committed and traced to the Quds Force of the Government of Iran. [Operation Red Coalition of the FBI publically revealed on October the 11th of 2011.]

There can be no question that it was another act of war planned by the Government of Iran, this one bold enough not to be surrounded by Iranian territory as it was in 1979– 1981, but within and surrounded by the United States. Other than charging those responsible and invoking more economic sanctions against Iran by the United States and continuing to fail at any meaningful U.N. resolutions, there was nothing done that would be retaliatory in nature.

Five months later [March the 14th of 2012] the Azerbaijan National Security Minister revealed that 22 persons connected to the Iranian Revolutionary Guard were arrested, being charged with plotting to attack the U.S. and Israeli Embassies in the capital city of Baku.

The consistent statement of the U.S. government that has stated "all options are on the table" does not frighten the government of Iran or other enemies of the United States because there always appears to be a reason why the most severe options that are "on the table" will simply be *left* "on the table" rather than using them.

The culture of U.S. diplomats is to use "smart" and "soft" diplomacy assuming it will be effective. But the culture of the adversaries of the U.S. is to perceive such smartness and softness as weakness and evidence that the U.S. is frightened.

Since ineffective resolutions and other diplomatic measures have been the continued preferred course taken by President Obama, and considering that tyrannies do not care about sanctions that hurt their people as long as their government is not damaged, there is one likely diplomatic course that could be effective in that, if passed or not passed, would bring harm and humiliation to the *government* rather than the people of Iran:

Article Six of the U.N. Charter states, "A member of the United Nations which has persistently violated the Principles contained in the present Charter may be expelled from the Organization by the General Assembly upon the recommendation of the Security Council." Therefore, with immense evidence, the United States could enter a resolution of Iran's expulsion for violations made since the Iranian Revolution began in 1979, by citing a litany of specifics in Articles One and

Two of the Charter that state the organization's Purposes and Principles.

Of course Russia and China would veto a Security Council resolution that would recommend the General Assembly take such a vote [which is the procedure], and even in the most unrealistic event that Russia and China would not enter vetoes, the General Assembly would likely vote overwhelmingly against it [with the probable abstention of most but not all Sunni Arab states]. But rejection and abstention would not be so certain if the United States first stated that if the resolution was not passed, the U.S. would eject *itself* from the United Nations. Without U.S. membership (and funds), the U.N. would die.

In short, the U.S. Ambassador to the U.N. should state that "if expulsion of Iran's government is not employed then the United States will have no moral choice but to resign from the U.N. for ignoring U.N. directives as recorded in the Charter." Or, dependent on the character of the U.S. Ambassador, putting it in blunt street-talk: "Take your choice. It's either Iran or the United States. As of tonight, you can't have both." If the Ayatollah Khamenei's government of Iran would not be ousted, then the delegates would have to give up their New York way of life—tonight. Prior to the vote, their government superiors back home would be swamped by messages from their U.N. representatives in New York justifying why they should be able to vote for the ejection of Iran.

In the interim, Iran's nuclear weapons capability was given an extraordinary amount of time to advance. Meaningful inspections by the International Atomic Energy Agency were denied. Then came an unprecedented publicly exposed policy: the United States was trying to convince Israel not to strike Iran's nuclear facilities. Israel was in danger of being annihilated in the likely period of time between the Iranian attempt to have operational nuclear weapons and the achievement of that objective. In obvious violation of the U.N.'s Charter against a fellow member of the U.N., Iran's President Mahmoud Ahmadinejad had already threatened that Israel must be "wiped off the map" [October the 26th of 2005] and his superior, the Ayatollah Khamenei said that Israel is a "cancerous tumor that should be cut, and will be cut." [February the 3rd of 2012.] Israel had already wiped out the partly constructed nuclear reactor of Iraq on June the 7th of 1981 and a partly constructed nuclear reactor in Syria on September the 6th of 2007, having been built with North Korean assistance.

Although likely for different reasons, Teheran and Washington D.C. were known to be on the same side in restraining Israel.

Because of this recent history and the continuing inaction of the United States in not doing much of anything other than seeming to have faith in writing worthless resolutions and sanctions and attempting to bring about talks, the Grand Ayatollah Khamenei and the officials of his revolutionary government must have been bewildered by the hesitancy of the United States to take a more meaningful course.

The Iranian opposition to its government was not bewildered by the hesitancy; it was horrified: *"Obama! Obama! Either You're with Them—or You're with Us!"*

SYRIA

The Iranian government's strongest ally was Syria's President Bashar al-Assad whose father, Hafez al-Assad, was President of Syria before him. It was not a well respected heritage of leadership because his father was best remembered for his 1982 slaughter of an estimated 10,000 to 25,000 citizens of the Syrian city of Hama who opposed his government. [That estimate was the one given by Amnesty International with its tremendous range between minimum and maximum figures necessary because, as could be assumed, there hadn't been an official estimate by the Syrian government.]

Thirty years later in 2012, Hafez al-Assad's son, Bashar, was competing with his father by massacring hundreds and then thousands of Syrian citizens with numbers expanding daily throughout the nation.

The protests had started slowly through Syrian streets in January of 2011 and gradually became larger while the world's eyes were on Egypt and not Syria. Before the events in Syria created world attention, U.S. Secretary of State Hillary Clinton said of Bashar al-Assad, "There's a different leader in Syria now. Many of the members of Congress of both parties who have gone to Syria in recent months have said they believe he's a reformer." [Excerpt from her appearance on NBC's *Meet the Press*: March the 27th 2011.] Although she did not say to whom she was referring, it was noticeable that she let the statement hang there without saying if the administration had a different opinion or agreed with it. Her reference to "many members of Congress" appeared to be the only member, Senator John Kerry, who had made a recent public statement. Eleven days earlier [on March the 16th] Senator Kerry said, "My judgment is that Syria will move, Syria will change as it embraces a legitimate relationship with the United States and the west, and economic opportunity that comes with it, and the participation that comes with it."

As the months went on, the protests against the government of Syria became more frequent and the reaction of Bashar al-Assad's government became more militant, increasing the number of casualties.

By February of 2012 when the toll of those killed reached 5,400, world governments exhibited interest. But only interest; not action against Bashar al-Assad. In the Syrian city of Homs with some one million residents, government forces used tanks and rockets and grenades and rifles, turning Homs into a citywide massacre.

The difference between the crimes of Bashar al-Assad's father and the crimes of his son was the technology that emerged in the thirty years between their atrocities. Now, despite most foreign reporters and photographers denied entry into Syria, some immensely brave citizens used their mobile phones with built-in cameras to record the terror, and then transmitted their pictures through social networks which were picked up on any number of internet sites for world-wide exhibition. That distribution was picked up by television sources with many broadcasters exerting sensitivity in blurring the most savage visuals of victims who had undergone absolute displayed horror.

If No-Fly Zones over Libya and air strikes against Qaddafi's forces had been effective in ending the perils of Benghazi, (and it was effective), why reject No-Fly Zones and air strikes to end the massacre of Homs, Syria? Instead, the Obama administration continued its pursuit of economic sanctions and attempts of diplomacy and U.N. resolutions. Syria's allies of Russia and China watered the resolutions down as soon as they were written, advocating more dialogue. But during the time-wasting pursuit, hell expanded.

According to residents of the city of Homs in Syria, often accompanied by confirming pictures, there were masses of corpses lying in the streets having been made victims only because they had been walking in those streets. Snipers were on rooftops and between buildings and there was barely a moment without blasts from rocket propelled grenades. There were quick burials held only at night so as not to be in view during daylight with mourners becoming victims of snipers, and there were other bodies waiting for burial while stored in apartments, homes, and shops. There was the destruction of Homs water-tower and the destruction of its major oil pipeline. There were reports of Red Cross vehicles targeted; doctors and nurses being forced out of hospitals; patients in operating rooms left with surgeries incomplete, along with other patients left to do nothing but suffer before life ended.

Death owned the residences, the businesses, the streets and the hospitals. In addition, most people of Homs were now living in a city without entrances or exits, with the government forces enforcing the closures so those not killed would be left to die and protest no more.

Russia and the People's Republic of China vetoed the next U.N. resolution against the al-Assad regime [February the 4th of 2012] even though those two governments had already watered down that resolution to such an extent that it hardly made much difference if it passed or didn't pass.

The White House stuck to its non-intervention policy, dismissing the idea of sending arms to the ill-supplied Free Syrian Army that was attempting to put down the al-Assad forces. If the U.S. unilaterally intervened or took the lead in an international intervention, it would put the U.S. in prime position of influence in a post al-Assad government.

President Obama told the press [February the 6th of 2012]. *"With respect to Syria, what's happening in Syria is heartbreaking and outrageous, and what you've seen is the international community mobilize against the Assad regime... For us to take military action, unilaterally, as some have suggested, or think that somehow there is some simple solution, I think is a mistake."*

On February the 7th of 2012, U.S. State Department Press Spokesperson Victoria Nuland was asked:

Q. Senator John McCain yet again this morning called for the United States to help arm the rebels, the insurgents, against the Assad government. Have you ruled this out?

A. Well, we never take anything off the table. The President does—doesn't. However, as far as the President himself made absolutely clear, and the Secretary has continued to say, we don't think more arms into Syria is the answer. We think the answer is to get to a national democratic dialogue, for the violence to stop, for the regime's tanks to come out of the cities, and then for monitors to be able to go back in.

Q. But they were the answer in Libya, weren't they?

A. Libya was a completely different situation.

Almost simultaneously at the White House, Jay Carney, Press Secretary of the President was holding his Daily Press Briefing in which he was asked:

Q. Senator Lieberman said it might be the time for the United States to get in the business of helping to arm the opposition and take more aggressive measures. Is that something that the administration is willing to consider?

A. I don't want to speculate. I believe we don't—we are not considering this step right now. We are exploring the possibility of providing humanitarian aid to Syrians and we are working with our partners, again, to ratchet up the pressure, ratchet up the isolation on Assad and his regime. We're seeing a lot of indications of a lack of control over the country by the regime, of interest by senior officials within the military and the government in separating themselves from the regime. So we believe that the pressure is having an impact. Ultimately, it needs to result in Assad ceasing the violence, stopping the brutality and allowing for a transition supported by the Syrian people.

Q. Thank you.

For those in Syria not knowing if they would last through day's end, and more important not knowing if the ones they love would last through day's end, the words from the White House that "we are not considering this step right now" told them the United States saw no urgency in keeping them alive. After all, President Obama's Press Secretary had said, "We're seeing a lot of indications of a lack of control over the country by the regime."

The estimates of those killed in Syria expanded from the 5,400 estimated in February to a U.N. figure of more than 9,000 as April began.

The current U.S. President was not repeating, either in speech or deed, the inaugural words of President John F. Kennedy: *"Let every nation know whether it wishes us well or ill, that we will pay any price, bear any burden, meet any hardship, support any friend and oppose any foe to assure the survival and the success of liberty."*

President Obama seemed to disagree with everything President Kennedy itemized within that statement.

8

BENEATH UNCERTAIN CLOUDS

AS THE CLOUDS of the storm over the Mediterranean and Middle East Theater moved over national borders, street protests of varying size and scope took place in other nations that were not immune from facing the same kind of fate taking place nearby. The edge of that storm was visible, with governments and people friendly to the United States more and more skeptical of U.S. support.

King Mohammed VI of Morocco and his father before him, King Hassan, had a long time tradition of ties to the United States but in 2011, in compliance with demands to have an earlier than scheduled election, Islamists received an unprecedented winning plurality.

Jordan's King Abdullah II's father, King Hussein [bin Talal], not only befriended the United States but led Jordan in being the second nation in the area [after Egypt under Sadat and retained by Mubarak] that gave diplomatic recognition to Israel with those relations retained by his son, King Abdullah II. Those agreements of recognition were made and retained although opposed by many other Arab States.

Sultan Qaboos of Oman is an incredible man for a host of policies during the Cold War and then in the current war, giving his own money (estimated to be $1,500,000) to rescue three American hikers who had been kept prisoners in Iran, and also sending an Omani aircraft to take them out of Iran to safety. It was not the first time he rescued American and other prisoners of Iran. He maintains a "cordial relationship" with Iran which gives him a unique rapport. In a strategic sense, the part of Oman that is separate from its major territory is the small tip of land [the peninsula of the Musandam Exclave] that juts out, sitting northeast of the United Arab Emirates, directly across from Iran with those two nations of Oman and Iran divided only by the Strait of Hormuz.

King Hamad of Bahrain has been hosting the Fifth Fleet of the United States Navy in an area of extreme volatility, and where that hosting has brought about, and continues to bring about, great risks for King Hamad from Iran across the Persian Gulf from Bahrain.

Those nations are monarchies; not democracies, but what must be considered are the alternatives to those governments. And what must also be considered is whether or not the United

States will be known as a loyal friend when an ally is under threat, or a nation that will reject the faithful.

Algeria led by President Abdelaziz Bouteflika, whose nation endured only a minimum of demonstrations, and has been an off-and-on friend of the United States through the years, has been facing elections in which there is a move for an alliance of Islamist parties for a coalition to form a majority. It is well known that there are those within some of that prospective coalition that have an allegiance to al-Qaeda.

Beyond the governments listed above, there are two nations that have recently seen armed conflicts:

"At the end of this year, America's military operation in Iraq will be over," President Obama said to the glee of adversaries of the United States who were seated in the U.N.'s General Assembly on September the 21st of 2011.

The reason for their glee was that they knew he had made his decision against the advice of his military advisors and against the advice of history in wars of the past when military forces were ordered to leave before achieving victory.

But what he said to the U.N. was accurate. During the early morning of December the 18th, 2011 the last of the U.S. troops did, indeed, leave Iraq. As President Obama was able to say in his next State of the Union Address: *"For the first time in nine years there are no Americans fighting in Iraq."* They had already crossed the border into the safety of Kuwait. Crossing that border would have meant nothing at all in 2011 if twenty years earlier, back in 1991, the United States and its coalition had left Kuwait before achieving victory in the liberation of Kuwait over what had been Iraq's conquest. But the U.S. and its allies won and did not leave until Kuwait was liberated.

In this case of 2011, the United States simply left the battle.

Libya was another country having been involved in immense armed conflict. Libya's leader for over 40 years was Muammar Qaddafi. [Qaddafi was the only leader whose name could be spelled correctly in English in at least eight different ways.] He had given himself the title of "The Leader" rather than any title other than "Colonel" or "Brotherly Leader." More accurately, President of Egypt Anwar Sadat had given Qaddafi the title of "a mental case; a nit-wit."

President Obama should be and has been justifiably praised for advocating and ordering U.S. forces to take part in the "No Fly Zone" and air strikes over Libya that prevented the slaughter of those Libyans living in the city of Benghazi. Further, his belief in a "No-Fly Zone" and air strikes was integral in the victory of Libyan fighters. For sure it was in the tradition of what Presidents Roosevelt, Truman, Eisenhower, Kennedy, Johnson, Nixon, Ford, Reagan, Bush (41), Clinton, and Bush (43) would have done.

What they would *not* have done was to become a *part* of a coalition of nations rather than being the *leader* of the coalition that directly brought about the end of the Muammar Qaddafi regime and brought about Qaddafi's demise. The phrase, "leading from behind" used by a White House advisor who preferred to be unmentioned by name, turned out to be the policy of the administration. Had the U.S. taken the lead, and have been proud of it, the United States could then have been influential and even instrumental in determining the government that would take over leadership, just as it was influential and instrumental decades back in Germany and Japan and other nations since then that became free. As of this writing, the cloud of a forthcoming Islamist government may leave the horizon of Libya with that nation untouched, or drizzle from the cloud may be a preview of the cloud's burst into a new Libyan storm.

In past decades, it was common for friends to feel that the United States would come to support them and, when necessary, the armed forces of the United States would be beside them. To this day, most people around the globe are aware that the United States liberated many millions of people and they can only imagine what the world would have been like if the U.S. hadn't entered World War II and the Cold War and Kuwait and Bosnia and Kosovo and how the world will likely look if the U.S. chooses to reject that role.

But better to imagine it rather than have the next generation live it.

9

ALONE

OBAMA ON ISRAEL: BORDERS "SHOULD BE BASED ON THE 1967 LINES"

On May the 19th of 2011 in a major address to the people of the world, President of the United States Barack Obama stated, *"We believe the borders of Israel and Palestine should be based on the 1967 lines with mutually agreed swaps, so that secure and recognized borders are established for both states."*

Unprecedented.

That statement regarding the 1967 lines is one of the worst, if not the very worst statement made by any U.S. President regarding a friendly nation that won a war.

Not even North Vietnam, a foe of the United States, has ever been told by a U.S. President to go back to the 1975 lines. Never. In 1975 North Vietnam won the territory of South

Vietnam after over 57,000 Americans died in a 13 year U.S. military engagement (1960–1973) to help the South Vietnamese retain its nation. In the years since the defeat, neither the United States nor any other nation has told North Vietnam to "give up that territory." There has been not one resolution to that effect offered in the United Nations. Instead, most countries of the world, including the United States, gave diplomatic relations and trade agreements with the Socialist Republic of Vietnam which is what *had* been known as North and South Vietnam.

In keeping with President Obama's Middle East policy, should the United States base its borders on the 1846 lines with Mexico? Or, for that matter base its lines of territory on the 1775 lines with Great Britain? How about with mutually agreed swaps?

What makes that line of his speech even more absurd is that a Palestinian state did not exist in 1967—or in any year—but certainly what he conveyed was that there was such a state in 1967.

Since, at the time of the President's speech, some 44 years had passed since the war, many people either forgot or never knew what happened back in 1967; some hadn't been born then or were too young to remember while some never learned the facts or simply forgot the facts in all the time that had passed.

Instead of what the President said, the war had nothing to do with the borders of the State of Israel and an Arab state called Palestine. It had, instead, *everything* to do with the imminent invasion from Arab States for the purpose of exterminating Israel:

On May the 18th, 1967, the Voice of the Arabs Radio broadcast that President Gamal Abdul Nasser of Egypt announced: "The sole method we shall apply against Israel is a total war which will result in the extermination of Zionist existence."

On May the 20th President Nasser instituted a blockade of the Gulf of Eilat so that no shipping could move in or out of Israel through the Red Sea. On the same date President Nasser's tanks started going eastward through the Sinai Desert toward Israel. Standing in the way of the tanks within the Sinai were the U.N. Emergency Force Peacekeepers. President Nasser asked Secretary General of the United Nations U Thant to remove the peacekeeping force as Nasser's tanks were about to invade Israel. In a move that defeated the purpose and even defeated the definition of a peacekeeping effort, Secretary General U Thant accommodated President Nasser and removed the U.N. Emergency Force peacekeepers so Nasser would be undeterred in launching his invasion.

On May the 27th Nasser said, "Our basic objective will be the destruction of Israel. The Arab people want to fight."

On May the 29th Nasser said, "We have reached the stage of serious action and not declarations."

On May the 30th Nasser said, "The armies of Egypt, Jordan, Syria and Lebanon are poised on the borders of Israel." Additionally, President Nasser stated publically that he had "received the commitment of Iraq's President Aref who announced, 'Our goal is clear—to wipe Israel off the map.'"

As May ended and June began, Nasser rejected a plea from the United States and European nations to "allow freedom of shipping in the Gulf of Aqaba" so war could be prevented. [The name, the Gulf of Aqaba is used in Arab nations while the name, the Gulf of Eilat is used in Israel. It's the same place.]

It is important to remember that the planned attack was not for the Sinai, not for the Gaza Strip, not for the Golan Heights, not for East Jerusalem, and not for Judea and Samaria. Egypt already had Sinai and the Gaza Strip, Syria already had the Golan Heights, Jordan already had East Jerusalem and had Judea and Samaria, having renamed those territories as their West Bank.

Israel was confident that at a minimum, Egypt's President Nasser and Syria's President Nureddin al-Atassi would order the invasion by their armed forces in a two-front war against Israel; Egypt from the south-west and Syria from the north. Israel's greatest concern was that Jordan would join them from the east in an attack for a three-front war.

Prime Minister Levi Eshkol of Israel wanted to guarantee to King Hussein of Jordan that if the King would just "sit on his hands and do nothing" when Egypt and Syria go to war against Israel, rather than join those two countries, "Israel will not attack or take one inch of any territory Jordan considers to be a part of its nation, including what Jordan calls its West Bank." But direct dialogue between Israel and Jordan was out of the question since diplomatic relations did not exist between them. Since Prime Minister Eshkol could not directly deliver the message to King Hussein, he communicated with the U.S. Ambassador to Israel, Ambassador Walworth Barbour, to see if he or Ambassador Findley Burns, Jr. the U.S. Ambassador to the Hashemite Kingdom of Jordan, would deliver Israel's message to King Hussein. [The United States had diplomatic relations with both Israel and Jordan.]

Ambassador Barbour did what all good U.S. Ambassadors do: he cabled the Secretary of State. The U.S. Secretary of State Dean Rusk brought the message to President Johnson.

President Johnson did one better than delegating Ambassador Barbour or Ambassador Burns to see King Hussein. He sent Under Secretary of State for Political Affairs Eugene Rostow from Washington, D.C. to be the President's envoy to visit with the King of Jordan and deliver a personal message from the President.

Secretary Rostow told King Hussein of the Israelis guarantee if the King would just "sit on his hands" rather than add a third front to the war against Israel. Secretary Rostow then added something more: not only did Israel make that guarantee if Jordan would not enter the war against Israel, but President Johnson for the *United States* would also guarantee that Israel would not take one inch of what Jordan considered to be its territory. "There is a promise of absolute immunity," Secretary Rostow told the King.

King Hussein gave no answer. At that time of his 31st year of life, the King wanted consent for such a decision, in this case permission from other Arab leaders including from Egypt's President Nasser. He didn't get it.

On Sunday, June the 4th, Egypt's Intelligence Agency informed Nasser of its analysis that Israel was getting ready to launch an attack on Egypt to preempt Egypt's planned invasion. In detail, Nasser was told that Israel was moving assault units and equipment to Eilat on the Gulf of Aqaba to stage that attack and they had observed that almost half of Israel's landing craft were being sent there.

Egypt's Intelligence Agency was correct in its assessment that the Israeli military was preparing Eilat. It was a logical site since Eilat was at the southern tip of the triangle of Israel between both Egypt and Jordan. On that southern tip of Israel, about four miles to Eilat's west was Taba in the Sinai of Egypt, and three miles to Eilat's east was Aqaba in Jordan. From Eilat, Israel could attack in either or both directions.

In response to the Egyptian intelligence report, Nasser ordered his combatants from the Mediterranean to come down to reinforce Arab naval strength in the Straits of Tiran off the coast of Eilat. But although the Israeli military was preparing Eilat, it was not being prepared as a launching site for attack. The buildup in Eilat was being staged as a decoy.

With an invasion of Israel having been announced by Egypt and by Syria and other Arab nations, and with Egyptian tanks coming across the Sinai toward Israel and with the Gulf of Eilat having been blockaded, Egypt was setting the time and place for the war. That was something Israel knew that, if allowed, Israel would likely not win. Victory could more likely be achieved if Israel could set the time and place. And it did.

On June the 5th Israel launched a preemptive strike, not from Eilat on Taba or Aqaba but from other sites in Israel targeting all of Egypt's airfields simultaneously, destroying almost the entire Air Force of Egypt, and striking Syrian and Iraqi military airfields while Israeli ground units began moving into the Gaza Strip and into the Sinai.

Israel was leaving Jordan and its West Bank alone and immune in the hope Jordan would "sit on its hands" as Secretary Rostow had offered King Hussein.

By the end of that first day of war King Hussein had not sat on his hands. The King's troops attacked Israel from its West Bank and East Jerusalem. Israel responded in moments by moving troops into Jordanian-held West Bank cities of Janin, Nablus, and the Jordanian-held sector of Jerusalem.

Six days after the war began, the war was over. All parties in the Mideast agreed to a U.N. cease-fire. It was apparent that Israel could have gone on to Cairo in Egypt, Damascus in Syria, and Amman in Jordan, but Israel accommodated the call for a cease-fire of the U.N. and, particularly, the encouragement of the United States to accept it since Israel had attained what they believed were now secure borders.

In those six days of war Israel had taken both the Gaza Strip and the entire Sinai Desert up to the Suez Canal from Egypt, and had taken the Golan Heights from Syria, and had taken all of Judea and Samaria (the West Bank) from Jordan including the Jordanian-held sector of Jerusalem.

Some two decades later, during the Reagan Administration, Eugene Rostow said that "the West Bank would still be held by Jordan today if King Hussein had accepted the offer from the U.S. and Israel."

But war's casualties were high, going into the tens of thousands including 34 Americans who were not killed by Egyptians or Syrians or Jordanians, but by Israelis who mistook the U.S. ship, U.S.S. Liberty, for a Soviet vessel aiding Egypt. That error was confirmed as friendly fire by ten U.S. investigations of the tragedy including a Naval Court of Inquiry in Malta. [Israel had been told three times by the U.S. Embassy in Tel Aviv that it is "Not our ship." The Embassy didn't think it was. It was later confirmed that it was an intelligence gathering ship with large radars visible off the coast of Sinai over 100 miles from the other ships of the U.S. Sixth Fleet.]

Because the losing Arab governments of the war were too dev-astated and humiliated to claim their loss was due to Israel's armed forces, they chose to blame the more powerful United States for their defeat. In making that claim, even Arab nations that were not militarily involved in the war severed diplomatic relations with the United States.

On June the 19th of 1967 President Johnson stated that going back to the pre-war borders as some Arab States were demand-ing, was *"not a prescription for peace, but for renewed hostilities."* But assume that what President Johnson said should be disregarded and, instead, borders should be based on the 1967 lines as President Obama has given as U.S. policy. Whether President Obama knew it or not, and maybe he didn't know it, that would not mean giving the territories to an Arab Palestinian state as President Obama suggested, but it would mean giving back the West Bank to Jordan who had invaded and seized it back in 1948 and it would mean giving the Gaza Strip back to Egypt who had invaded and took jurisdiction over it also back in 1948, neither nation even wanting those territories in years following the 1967 War for the following reasons:

Three years after the 1967 war King Hussein fought a war not from a threat from Israel but from a war against the Pal-estine Liberation Organization (PLO) of Yasser Arafat who wanted to take over Jordan.

[The PLO wanted to take over all of Jordan as well as what Jordan had called the West Bank but had once again been named Judea and Samaria since it was back in Israel's hands since winning the 1967 war.] The PLO was aided by Syria and Iraq; a war in which King Hussein's Jordanian troops killed an estimated 10,000 members and supporters of the PLO and drove Yasser Arafat to Lebanon where he started "a state within a state." During that war King Hussein requested aid from the United States, Great Britain, and from Israel, with all three nations accommodating King Hussein. During his lifetime, King Hussein survived 12 assassination attempts by what were becoming referred to as Arab Palestinians.

Egypt was also disillusioned with Arab Palestinians, and in 1978 President Anwar Sadat at Camp David talks with U.S. President Carter and Israel's Prime Minister Begin, Sadat made no demand to have the Gaza Strip once again be under Egypt's jurisdiction. Instead, he agreed to an ambiguous future autonomy. There was never any secret that due to so many of Gaza's radical inhabitants and its leadership, President Sadat considered the Gaza Strip a territorial burden rather than a prized Egyptian jurisdiction. [It was three rulers earlier when Egyptian King Farouk had seized control of the Gaza Strip in the 1948 War.] Sadat had been stuck with it.

OBAMA: "OCCUPATION"

Throughout the Obama Administration, the U.S. Government called the West Bank and the Gaza Strip as land "occupied by Israel." In his major speech on the Middle East given on May the 19th of 2011 President Obama once more spoke of Israel as an occupier. He said, *"The dream of a Jewish and democratic state cannot be fulfilled with permanent occupation."*

The unasked but obvious question was how the Arab Palestinians in the West Bank and the Gaza Strip could claim their land was occupied when they never had that land? It was a question never referred to by President Obama as he persisted in calling it an Israeli occupation. Before the June War of 1967 when Egypt had jurisdiction over the Gaza Strip and Jordan had taken the West Bank, neither Egypt nor Jordan were called "occupiers." During its nineteen years of jurisdiction neither Egypt nor Jordan would allow its citizens to even mention the words, "independent Palestinian state."

Before Jordan and Egypt, Great Britain had jurisdiction over that land. And before that it was under the jurisdiction of the Ottoman Empire of Turkey. And before that was the time of the Crusades and before that Rome ruled it. And that takes the calendar back to Biblical times.

The only period that could even be perceived as an interruption of jurisdictions was the U.N.'s designation of an independent Arab state for portions of Judea and Samaria and Gaza, but it never came to fruition because of the instant invasion, seizure and jurisdiction by Jordan over Judea and Samaria and by Egypt over Gaza during the quests of Jordan and Egypt to seize Israel.

Palestine was never a nation but a region much as Scandinavia is not a nation but is a region containing the nations of Denmark, Norway, and Sweden. Through the years the definition of Palestine's territory went through a myriad of boundaries, partitions, and changes of borders. The original Mandate for Palestine [April 24, 1920] included what today is called Jordan,

Israel, the West Bank, and Gaza. Divided into percentages it would have been 78% to Jordan, and all the rest would have been 22%. (Taking away what today is called the West Bank and Gaza from Israel would then give Israel 17½%.) By the time of U.N. Resolution 181 [November 29, 1947] borders had been changed to make Jordan a separate state not included in Palestine. [During all this time Jordan was called Transjordan. Its name was changed in 1949 to the Hashemite Kingdom of Jordan.] Jerusalem was designated to be an international zone which Jordan did not permit.

On May 14, 1948, Israel declared its independence in compliance with the borders prescribed in U.N. Resolution 181. When Egypt and Jordan then went to war to take all the land Egypt and Jordan did not receive by the U.N., Jordan got as far as seizing East Jerusalem and taking over Judea and Samaria. All Jews who survived the Jordanian invasion were either killed or expelled. Their graveyards were all that were left of them and so they were destroyed, with the gravestones used as latrines. Christians who remained were mandated to send their children to schools to learn the Islamic religion. Even with the failure of seizing Israel, there was triumph in Jordan's success in taking Judea, Samaria, and East Jerusalem in the 1948 War and in Egypt's jurisdiction over the Gaza Strip, and both Jordan and Egypt retained the belief that a forthcoming war would give those Arab Nations possession of Israel-proper.

It is apparent that the term "occupation" has recently been used to describe what *friends* of the United States do when they win wars, but not *enemies* of the United States do when they win wars. Not just Vietnam: the State Department would later try to bring about a partition of Bosnia that had been captured in horrible acts of aggression by Slobodan Milosevic's Serbia. The U.S. did not refer to Milosevic's capture as occupied territory, but as "facing the fact that it won those territories in war."

OBAMA AND "THE RIGHT OF RETURN"

Most Arab leaders insist on the refugees in their camps be given what they call the "Right of Return" to Israel: In 1948 a number of Arab governments; Lebanon, Syria, Jordan and Egypt, told those Arabs who lived in the land that had now been designated by the U.N. as Israel, to leave that land and come to those Arab countries for a short stay until another war would be launched against Israel and result in Arab victory, and the Arabs who had lived there could then return. In 1948 there were an estimated figure of somewhere between 650,000 and 750,000 Arabs who left Israel at the urging of those Arab governments. When they arrived they were put in refugee camps of those Arab nations. Those still living from 1948, and many of their descendants, are still there.

In most cases those in camps have not been allowed to integrate in the Arab countries in which the refugee camps were and remain located. As generations went on, Arab leaders claimed four to five million refugees. That is certainly possible since these Arabs are mainly generations descending from those who came in 1948. If all those currently considered refugees were to go to Israel under the "Right of Return," Israel would become the 23rd Arab nation.

In the year of President Obama's May 19 speech, 2011, the population of Israel was approximately 7,500,000 including approximately 1,200,000 Arabs living in Israel, many being descendants from those Arabs who elected to stay in Israel in 1948 rather than go to an Arab State as they were told to do by Arab leaders. With some four to five million estimated "returning refugees" from Arab nations, Arabs would then most likely become the majority population of Israel.

Of course the Arab Palestinian leadership could have invited them into the areas of the West Bank that Israel gave the Palestinian Authority after the Oslo Accords of 1993 and to the Gaza Strip in which Arab Palestinians have held total jurisdiction since Israel's Prime Minister Sharon's directive of 2005 giving the Gaza Strip to them.

The United Nations Agency Relief and Works Agency (UNRWA) for Palestinian Refugees in the Near East states that the refugees in those camps in Arab nations "do not 'own' the land on which their shelters were built, but have the right to 'use' the land for a residence. Socio-economic conditions in the camps are generally poor, with high population density, cramped living conditions and inadequate basic infrastructure such as roads and sewers. UNRWA's responsibility in the camps is limited to providing services and administering its installations. The Agency does not own, administer or police the camps as this is the responsibility of the host authorities."

At this writing, there are 58 Arab Palestinian Refugee Camps. To the great credit of the Hashemite Kingdom of Jordan, in contrast to its Arab neighbors, Jordan has treated those from the camps in Jordan as equals and not as inferior, with Jordan allowing and encouraging integration among Jordan's citizenry beyond the refugee camps. Since King Abdulluh I [the first King of the Hashemite Kingdom,] Jordanians and Palestinians were considered one and the same people, and the term Palestinian has not officially been used as a point of separation. That has continued through all Jordan's following Kings; Talal, Hussein, and Abdulluh II.

During the 2008 U.S. presidential campaign, Senator Obama stated his opposition to the Arab Palestinians claim of the "Right of Return" with his position of opposition applauded in the United States. Those statements of his opposition were not repeated after he became President. Instead, any time the issue came up he relegated the issue to later negotiations or determination. Because of the scope and importance of the May 19th, 2001 speech, the absence of mentioning such a critical issue in that speech was apparent.

OBAMA: "NEGOTIATIONS SHOULD RESULT IN TWO STATES"

In the President Obama's May the 19th speech, he said, *"The United States believes that negotiations should result in two states, with permanent Palestinian borders with Israel, Jordan, and Egypt, and permanent Israeli borders with Palestine."* Assuming that Palestine is to be a state, why didn't he also say permanent Israeli borders with Jordan, Egypt, Lebanon and Syria? That does not mean he intended to leave out those borders but he was even leaving out territory on pre-war maps of 1967.

The phrase, "a two state solution with two states living side by side in peace and security" has been used in one way or another countless times by the President and spokespeople of the State Department, becoming the memorized statement to answer almost any question regarding U.S. policy toward Israel. In the General Assembly of the United Nations on September the 23rd of 2009, President Obama said, *"The goal is clear: two states living side by side in peace and security."* On August the 20th of 2010 Secretary of State Hillary Clinton in a State Department Press Briefing put it this way: "The goal of two states—Israel and Palestine, living side by side in peace and security." On May the 17th of 2011 in a meeting with King Abdullah II of Jordan in the Oval Office, President Obama said, *"two states that are living side by side in peace and security."* But a clear indication that such a plan would not bring about peace and security is that thousands of missiles had already been launched from the Gaza Strip against Israel ever since the Gaza Strip had been completely withdrawn by Israel when Israel's Prime Minister Ariel Sharon forced out the over 9,000 Israelis who lived there in 2005 and gave the entire Gaza Strip to the Palestinian Authority in the hope it would attain that peace and security. It attained neither. During the next six years 18,000 missiles were launched from the Gaza Strip into Israel. Those missiles were sent from Iran and Syria to their surrogates of Hamas in Gaza and also to Hezbollah in Lebanon, being used as a storage depot for what might conceivably be their later use in another war against Israel.

There is a tremendous global inconsistency in U.S. foreign policy that should be apparent as the United States advocates a *Two State Solution* for Israel and the Palestinian Authority while in another international controversy, the U.S. advocates a *One State Solution* for Taiwan and the People's Republic of China. In the Middle East the state of Israel is a long time friend of the United States and a democracy, yet is told to give land to a foe of the United States: Arab Palestinians in a Two State Solution. In Asia, the state of Taiwan is a long time friend of the United States and a democracy, yet is told that because of the United States "One China policy" Taiwan has no right to exist as a nation: "There is One China; the People's Republic of China, and Taiwan is part of China." Friends of the United States have to pay the price—in one case by the U.S. policy of a Two State Solution and in the other case by the U.S. policy of a One State Solution.

OBAMA DOING "WHAT HAS LONG BEEN ACKNOWLEDGED PRIVATELY"

Three days after President Obama's statement on the 1967 borders, he said to the 2011 AIPAC Conference [the American Israeli Political Affairs Committee], *"What I did on Thursday was to say publicly what has long been acknowledged privately. I've done so because we can't afford to wait another decade, or another two decades, or another three decades to achieve peace."* [May the 22nd of 2011] If that is true, did he find out why any of those who said it privately didn't say it publically?

While no evidence was given of those who advocated using the 1967 lines said it privately, there is evidence that there were statements by U.S. Presidents from the 1967 war forward who did not want an independent Palestinian state *at all*, even including President Carter [who became an anti-Israel voice and author of *"Palestine Peace Not Apartheid"* after leaving the Presidency, but not while occupying the office of the Presidency]:

While President, on August the 10th, 1979, President Carter said, "I am against any creation of a separate Palestinian state. I don't think it would be good for the Palestinians. I don't think it would be good for Israel. I don't think it would be good for the Arab neighbors of such a state." His statement was consistent with Presidents Johnson, Nixon, and Ford, the three other Presidents since the 1967 War, except that President Carter for the first time added: "I don't think it would be good for the Arab neighbors of such a state." The mystery of what he meant was solved twenty days later.

In a Question and Answer Session with Florida Newspaper Editors in Tampa on August the 30th of 1979, President Carter went further: "I have never met an Arab leader that in private professed a desire for an independent Palestinian state. Publicly, they all espouse an independent Palestinian state, almost all of them, because that is what they committed themselves to do at Rabat. But the private diplomatic tone of conversations is much more proper than is often alleged by the press and by others. Really, it would be a very great surprise to me for Crown Prince Fahd to send through our Ambassador, John West, to me a message: 'If you don't expedite the resolution of the Palestinian question, we will cut off your oil.'"

On September the 9th, 1979, President Anwar Sadat of Egypt was the guest on the NBC television program, *Meet the Press*. His honesty trapped him into saying something he had not planned on saying. The host of the Sunday show, Bill Monroe, asked President Sadat an unexpected question: "Mister President, President Carter says that when he talks privately with Arab leaders, they tell him they do not want an independent Palestinian state. Do you agree with that? Is that your experience as well?"

President Sadat was surprised by the question. He hesitated and then answered, "It is a family business and I choose better to abstain."

There was no question about what President Sadat was confirming. Now the secret would be known throughout the world if major media headlined it. They didn't. In the week following the interview, the State Department breathed a sigh of relief as President Sadat's statement went largely unnoticed.

On February the 25th of 1980, President Carter added to previous revelations: "I am opposed to an independent Palestinian state because in my own judgment and in the judgment of many leaders in the Middle East, including Arab leaders, this would be a destabilizing factor in the Middle East and would certainly not serve the United States interests."

President Ronald Reagan said on September the 1st of 1982 in his address to the nation: "In the pre-1967 borders Israel was barely 10 miles wide at its narrowest point. The bulk of Israel's population lived within artillery range of hostile Arab armies. I am not about to ask Israel to live that way again."

But years later there was a non-visionary concept of "Land for Peace" that was prescribed at the 1991 Madrid Peace Conference, meaning land from Israel for Arab Palestinians, and in return Israel would receive peace. The Madrid Peace Conference was hosted by U.S. President George H. W. Bush (41) and President Mikhail Gorbachev of the Soviet Union. Probably not by intention but in time the "Land for Peace" designation given in Madrid became a three word disguise since the land had to first be given up by Israel before the promised peace by Arab Palestinians. Moreover, the opposite of "peace" is "war"; not "land." By the use of the words given it was obvious that land would be attempted to be seized by war if it wasn't given away by peace. Whether individuals knew it or not, the United States endorsement of "Land for Peace" was based on the premise of rewarding the party threatening war.

Assume that Mexico becomes a strong military force in the future and Mexico's President demands the return of "occupied territory of the North Bank" from the United States. Should the U.S. President offer Land for Peace? Or assume that you live in a neighborhood where gangs inhabit most of the residences. Would you accept an offer to give up one of the rooms of your residence for their promise of peace?

Bill Clinton was the next President of the United States. During his administration his wife, Hillary Clinton, made a statement of support for an independent Arab Palestinian state but President Clinton put an arm's length between him and what she had said. President Clinton's Press Secretary, Mike McCurry, immediately stated, "That view expressed personally by the First Lady is not the view of the President." President Clinton, however, did support the Oslo Accords which were officially signed on September the 13th of 1993 on the White House South Lawn by Palestine Liberation negotiator, Mahmoud Abbas and Israeli Foreign Minister Shimon Peres, witnessed by U.S. President Bill Clinton, U.S. Secretary of State Warren Christopher, Palestine Liberation Organization Chairman Yasser Arafat, Israeli Prime Minister Yitzhak Rabin, and Foreign Minister of Russia, Andrei Kozyrev.

The Oslo Accords [The Oslo Declaration of Principles on Interim Self-Government Arrangements] gave an affirmation of the "Land for Peace" interpretation by Arab States of U.N. Resolution 242 of November 22, 1967 [see below]. That support of the Oslo Accords was, beyond argument, President Clinton's de-facto support of an independent Arab state. [Under the Oslo

Accords, Israel agreed to give 40% of the Gaza Strip and to give Jericho on the West Bank followed by Nablus, Ramallah, Janin, Bethlehem, Hebron, Tulkarm, and Qalqilya to start.]

On October the 2nd of 2001 President George W. Bush (43) did, in fact, give approval of an Arab Palestinian state. He said, "the idea of a Palestinian state has always been part of a vision, so long as the right of Israel to exist is respected." Not the vision of President Johnson. Not the vision of President Nixon. Not the vision of President Ford. Not the vision of President Carter. Not the vision of President Reagan. It had only been the vision of President Bush (41) as well as the actions of President Clinton. Before the 1967 War, while Jordan and Egypt held the territories during the administrations of Truman, Eisenhower, and Kennedy, it was not an issue as during those administrations it had become an accepted international fact that Jordan and Egypt won those territories in the 1948 war. Had those nations wanted an independent state during those nineteen years they would not have invaded and seized those territories in 1948 but simply called those territories an independent Arab state as the U.N. had prescribed.

U.N. RESOLUTIONS 242 AND 338

Just as the staff of United States Government bureaucracies have a fetish of speaking in acronyms and initials in the belief they are raising their prestige among people who don't know what they're talking about, those who deal in foreign policy supersede that eccentricity with a passion for numbers. They like to talk about a G8 Summit, and a meeting with the P5 +1, and 6 Party Talks, and what the Quartet is doing.

Barely a day has passed that the U.N. has been in session since the end of 1967 forward that someone hasn't let the numbers 242 and [years later, 338] roll out of their mouths in proof of their knowledge of U.N. Resolutions by numbers alone without stating what was said in those resolutions. We can be certain that 242 will come up again without definition. The Obama Administration has long supported Resolution 242 as though Resolution 242 directs Israel to give up all it had won in 1967, directing that the borders should be based on the 1967 lines. It doesn't direct that. There is certainly no problem in supporting 242 but it has to be known what 242 really says and what 242 doesn't say:

On November 22, 1967, five and one-half months after the Six Day War of 1967, the United Nations passed Resolution 242. Its most important statement was the declaration of "withdrawal of Israeli armed forces from territories of recent conflicts." What Arab diplomats and their allies hoped would be forgotten was that there was an absence of the word "the" or "all" preceding the words "territories of recent conflicts." Before the approval of Resolution 242 Arab States wanted the word "the" and the Soviet Union wanted the word "all." The United States and the United Kingdom insisted neither of those two words be used. The U.S. and the U.K. won. Therefore, the written and approved resolution called only for withdrawal "from territories" not stating which territories, how many, or how much of them. It meant that Israel must give up somewhere from .01% to 100% of the territories. Eleven years later, Israel could have claimed that it was acting in full compliance of U.N. Resolution 242 by signing the 1978 Camp David Accords returning Sinai to Egypt. In giving up Sinai, Israel gave up 92% of the territories gained in that war.

UN Resolution 338 was a reaffirmation of Resolution 242: [" . . . the implementation of Security Council Resolution 242 in all its parts"] and a call for a cease-fire in the Yom Kippur War of 1973, which had been launched against Israel by Egypt and Syria and aided by seven other Arab States. Resolution 338 also included a call for the start of negotiations between the parties. It was adopted on October 22 of 1973, some six days before the end of the Yom Kippur War.

OBAMA: "A SOVEREIGN AND CONTIGUOUS STATE"

"The Palestinian people must have the right to govern themselves, and reach their full potential, in a sovereign and contiguous state" was said in President Obama's May 19th speech. That passed by many listeners unnoticed.

He had said it earlier on September the 23rd of 2009 when he told the United Nations that he wants *"a viable Palestinian State with contiguous territory that ends the occupation of 1967."*

Contiguous, of course, means connecting without interruption. The Gaza Strip is in the southwest and the West Bank is in the east, and in order to connect them into a contiguous area, there needs to be land carved out of what has been Israel since its independence in 1948, going even well beyond the 1967 lines. This would need to be done by either giving the Arab Palestinian state a connecting road and/or railroad and/or some other currently Israeli land so as to make those two Arab Palestinian territories connected.

Therefore, President Obama's *"must have"* goal would make Israel *non*-contiguous.

"Over the last three years as President of the United States I have kept my commitments to the state of Israel at every crucial juncture! At every fork in the road! We have been there for Israel every single time!" [March the 4th of 2012]

One glance at a map reveals that such a connection of an Arab Palestinian state would not only have to cut Israel in two but the new Palestinian strip would be an ideal launching area from which to attack Israel on either side of the Arab Palestinian link of contiguity.

It is entirely possible that President Obama was not aware of the factual history of those events in the Middle East that preceded his administration, nor the inherent dangers in his plan for the future of the area. No matter the reason for his beliefs, President Obama was pursuing policies dismissive of another U.S. *Special Relationship.*

10

THE WEST ASIAN THEATER

AFGHANISTAN AND PAKISTAN

Vice President Joe Biden said, "Look, the Taliban per se is not our enemy. That's critical. There is not a single statement that the President has ever made in any of our policy assertions that the Taliban is our enemy because it threatens U.S. interests." [Excerpt from the Vice President's interview in *Newsweek*: December the 15th of 2011.]

To those who knew Joe Biden it was not surprising. He often made outrageous statements; he always did them with conviction; he was known as being fun to be with exhibiting a great sense of humor—and he was wrong with great frequency regarding foreign policy throughout his earlier Senatorial career: he opposed aid to South Vietnam although the U.S., in writing, had promised aid in case of North Vietnamese aggression; he opposed President Reagan's Strategic Defense Initiative for a U.S. method of striking down incoming missiles; he endorsed the Soviet demanded Nuclear Freeze; he opposed the Trans-Alaska Pipeline; he endorsed the "Peace Dividend" in cutting U.S. defense appropriations; he opposed President George H.W. Bush's military liberation of Kuwait from its takeover by Iraq; he advocated that Iraq be split into three nations of Shia, Sunni, and Kurd; and he opposed the major surge of U.S. troops in Iraq.

But this new statement regarding the Taliban was made not as a Senator from Delaware but as Vice President of the United States, and it was highly unlikely that he would make such a statement without echoing the feeling of the President. The public confirmation it was the policy of the President came five and one-half months later on May the 1st of 2012 when President Obama announced that *"In coordination with the Afghan government, my Administration has been in direct discussions with the Taliban."*

Could it not be remembered that the Taliban had been the host government of al-Qaeda in the Islamic Republic of Afghanistan, sheltering and housing al-Qaeda while, among countless acts of terrorism, al-Qaeda was planning and executing the 9-11 attacks on the United States? Not an enemy of the United States? What does it take?

One month after 9-11, President Bush (43), along with the British and with groups of Afghans including the Northern Alliance, launched a military attack against the Taliban government. In just 37 days [from October the 7th through November the 13th of 2001,] the Taliban was deposed, falling from the reins of government and fleeing to caves and border areas, but sustaining its existence under the continuing leadership of Mullah Omar.

Paramount in all this was the importance of the state of the Islamic Republic of Pakistan that bordered Afghanistan and was needed by the United States as a military supply line into Afghanistan. That brought about an international marriage of convenience between the United States and Pakistan; not a marriage of love.

From the beginning, Pakistan was known to be an untrustworthy partner. After all, forgotten by many was that the Taliban was not bred and born in Afghanistan. It was bred and born in Pakistan:

In a scarcely noticed incursion from Pakistan, the Taliban entered Afghanistan little by little in late 1994 and early 1995, coming across the border appearing to be little more than a joke. It was a group of several thousand kids launched by former students at Islamic seminaries in Pakistan. They were largely teen-agers and those in their early twenties who called themselves the Taliban, meaning "the seekers" and described as "religious students." That group's movement into Afghanistan was, however, supported by Pakistan's Fundamentalist Assembly of Islamic Clergy and by the better-known ISI [standing for the Inter Services Intelligence Agency or, more formally, the Inter-Services Intelligence Branch of Pakistan's Army.]

At first they took small villages, then larger villages, then small cities, then larger cities. The kids were no longer taken lightly as they captured the city of Kandahar. And after that victory they had enough prestige to garner more Afghan followers. With a larger force they then managed to take territory all the way to Jalalabad. That conquest occurred on September the 11th of 1996, which became an anniversary that was often referred to before and after 9-11 of 2001, five years to the day after their triumph in overtaking Jalalabad.

Two weeks after taking Jalalabad came the fall of Kabul, the capital city. That gave them the government.

They established a ruling council of six men, (a Shura) with a supreme commander whose appearance was not like any other member of the council, or for that matter any other Pakistani: He was Mullah Mohammed Omar with a height of 6' 6" with one eye missing. [The Taliban had previously given him the Islamic title of Amir-ul Momineen, that title acknowledging him as the undisputed head of the jihad or holy war.]

The Taliban immediately imposed strict Sharia law and ordered that all girls must leave school with a prohibition on their return. Girls and women were no longer allowed to be educated at all, or allowed to work. If able to be seen in public they were instructed to be dressed in the covering of a full-length burqa including a chadri headdress with only eyes exposed behind a screened horizontal slit.

Other than Islam no other religion was allowed to be practiced under the Taliban. No Christian Churches were left standing, nor any other places of non-Islamic religious practice. The huge statues of Buddha carved into a Bamiyan Valley mountainside some 1700 years earlier were dynamited into destruction. The Foreign Minister said, "We would not like to have them anymore."

Since the Taliban took over Kabul, on Fridays crowds of people went to the outdoor stadium southwest of the Ministry of Justice to watch convicted criminals being doomed to their punishments. Women guilty of what the Taliban interpreted as promiscuity were brought to the center of the stadium and killed by either being stoned to death or being shot in the back of their heads. Men convicted of thievery had their arms cut off and those convicted of more serious crimes often had their throats slit.

For the rest of Afghanistan's citizens there was nothing that could be defined as any diversion from the horrors of the government. International news was forbidden, theaters had been closed and all television sets, VCR's, and satellite dishes were prohibited by law by the Minister for the Prevention of Vice and the Promotion of Virtue.

As soon as Kabul was under Taliban control, Pakistan was the first nation to give diplomatic recognition to the Taliban as the legal government of Afghanistan.

On December the 1st of 2009 President Obama told the nation in an address, *"In the past we too often defined our relationship with Pakistan narrowly. Those days are over. Moving forward, we are committed to a partnership with Pakistan that is built on a foundation of mutual interest, mutual respect, and mutual trust. We will strengthen Pakistan's capacity to target those groups that threaten our countries, and have made it clear that we cannot tolerate a safe-haven for terrorists whose location is known, and whose intentions are clear."*

But not true. The foundation never had mutual interest, respect, or trust. And for sure Pakistan was maintaining safe-havens for terrorists whose locations were not only known but were maintained and guarded by Pakistanis friendly to both al-Qaeda and the Taliban.

THE RAID ON OSAMA BIN LADEN IN PAKISTAN

Beyond a doubt, President Obama made a wise and courageous decision in determining to give the go-ahead for the team of U.S. Navy Seal Team Six to stage a raid on Osama bin Laden, whose living quarters had been discovered in Pakistan. Since 2005 Osama bin Laden had been living in Abbottabad, Pakistan in a large and guarded compound estimated to be worth $1,000,000, some 35 miles north of the capital city of Islamabad and only one-half mile from Pakistan's major military academy.

After meeting with his advisors, President Obama gave the "go" to what became the May 1st, 2011 raid.

In excerpts from Vice President Joe Biden [on January the 30th of 2012 to ABC News Radio], when President Obama asked his top advisers on whether he should give a 'go' or 'no-go' to the prospective raid, "Every single person in that room hedged their bet except Leon Panetta. [Leon Panetta was Director of the Central Intelligence Agency at the time.] Leon said 'go.' Everyone else said '49 / 51.'

"He got to me. He said, 'Joe, what do you think?' And I said, 'You know, I didn't know we had so many economists around the table.' I said, "We owe the man a direct answer. Mister President, my suggestion is 'don't go.' We have to do two more things to see if he's there."

According to the Vice President, the President wanted to sleep on it and some 16 hours later the President directed his National Security Advisor, Tom Donilon, to give the 'go' for the raid. Osama bin Laden was killed.

There was relief expressed along with thanks to the Presi-

dent particularly by those who had been touched by the killings of thousands in terrorist attacks ordered by Osama bin
Laden. In truth, almost every American in one way or another
was touched by those attacks along with so many others around
the world.

President Obama's decision was reminiscent of the exception to the foreign policy record of President Carter who, as
stated earlier, courageously ordered an attempt to rescue the
U.S. hostages held in Iran. He did that against the advice of
top advisors including his Secretary of State Cyrus Vance who
resigned that office in his anger over the President's decision
to go ahead with the rescue attempt. The attempt [Operation
Eagle Claw] failed through a series of events during the mission, ending when one of the helicopters being used crashed
into a transport plane also being used in the attempt, resulting
in the death of eight U.S. servicemen.

Success or failure, those decisions of both President Carter
in 1980 and President Obama in 2011 took the reins of Commander in Chief by doing what was right against an enemy,
performing what President Kennedy had called the "stuff of
Presidents" without the approval or consultation with the
Congress.

It should be noted that Vice President Biden was truly admi-
rable in publically confessing that he opposed what became the
best foreign policy decision of the Obama Administration. He
did, however, perhaps go somewhat over the top in a little too
much exuberance at a fundraiser for an Obama-Biden second
term [March the 20th of 2012] when he referred to the raid on
Abbottabad by saying, "You can go back 500 years. You cannot find a more audacious plan." Since that takes the calendar

back to the year 1511 and through every year thereafter until the raid on Abbottabad, it is not too difficult to think of some events that might be considered competitors.

Director of the Central Intelligence Agency [CIA] Leon Panetta proved himself as being more than worthy of being an advisor in speaking up as he did when President Obama asked for advice, knowing no one else was giving a direct answer to the President's question other than Vice President Biden whose advice was contrary to his own.

Two days after the raid, [May the 3rd] Brian Williams interviewed Director Panetta on the *NBC Nightly News,* and during the interview Director Panetta was asked by Brian Williams: "I'd like to ask you about the sourcing on the Intel that ultimately led to this successful attack. Can you confirm that it was, uh, as a result of water boarding that we learned what we needed to learn to go after bin Laden?"

Director Panetta answered: "You know, Brian, in the intelligence business you work from a lot of sources of information and that was true here. We had a multiple source—a multiple series of sources—that provided information with regards to the situation. Clearly some of it came from detainees and the interrogation of detainees but we also had information from other sources as well: from secret intelligence, from imagery, from other sources that—we had—assets on the ground—and it was a combination of all of that, that ultimately we were able to put together, that led us to that compound. So it's a little difficult to say it was due just to one source of information that we got."

Brian Williams asked the question in different words: "Turned around the other way, are you denying that water boarding was in part among the tactics used to extract the intelligence that led to this successful mission?"

Leon Panetta answered, "No. I think some of the detainees uh, clearly uh, were uh—you know, they used these enhanced interrogation techniques against some of these detainees but I'm also saying that, you know the debate about whether we would have gotten the same information through other approaches I think is always going to be an open question."

Brian Williams responded with "So - finer point—one final time: enhanced interrogation techniques which has always been kind of a handy euphemism in these post 9-11 years— that includes water boarding?"

"That's correct."

Few, if any other Obama Administration officials, including the President himself, had ever given statements that would give public credit to George W. Bush and Bush's administration for the use of enhanced interrogation techniques that likely made the raid possible and successful.

Prior to the Abbottabad mission, President Obama nominated Leon Panetta to be his Secretary of Defense. Leon Panetta was confirmed by the Senate and became Secretary of Defense on July the 1st of 2011.

AFTER BIN LADEN

There was a sad and revealing epilogue to all this in that thousands of Pakistanis staged demonstrations against the U.S. raid that killed Osama bin Laden. In addition and even more revealing was the reaction of the government of Pakistan. Both President Asif Ali Zardari and Prime Minister Syed Yousef Raza Gilani made a series of angry statements against the United States for "infringing on the sovereignty of Pakistan" by staging the raid in Abbottabad. But that begs the questions, even for diplomats, that if they really thought it was an infringement on Pakistan's sovereignty for the United States to stage that raid, was it not a far greater infringement of Pakistan's sovereignty by Osama bin Laden and his people to be living in Abbottabad for over five years and likely having journeyed for an earlier four years through other areas of Pakistan searching for a secure compound?

If Pakistan could not rid Osama bin Laden from such a stay and residence, why not celebrate the United States for riding bin Laden's infringement on their sovereignty? Unless, of course, bin Laden was there at the invitation of Pakistan itself, or at least was not thought to be a threat to its security. If the United States and Pakistan were allies against al-Qaeda terrorists, how could that partnership bring about success if one of the two partners secretly harbored al-Qaeda's leader? Neither President Zardari nor Prime Minister Gilani protested when President Obama made the December the 1st, 2009 statement that *"we are committed to a partnership with Pakistan that is built on a foundation of mutual interest, mutual respect, and mutual trust. We will strengthen Pakistan's capacity to target those groups that threaten our countries, and have made it clear that we cannot tolerate a safe-haven for terrorists whose location is known, and whose intentions are clear."*

Soon the government of Pakistan imprisoned five Pakistanis who were charged with aiding United States CIA agents locate the compound of Osama bin Laden for the strike of the U.S. Navy Seals. One of those who had been arrested for being an informant for the CIA was Dr. Shikal Afridi who months after the arrests, was charged with treason for attempting to get information for the CIA's mission. On January the 29th of 2012 it was acknowledged by Defense Secretary Panetta that Dr. Shikal Afridi did, indeed, aid the CIA in the lead-up to the raid. "I'm very concerned . . . " the Secretary of Defense said in an excerpt from an interview on *60 Minutes* of CBS News, "This was an individual who, in fact, helped provide intelligence that was very helpful with regards to the operation. And he was not in any way treasonous towards Pakistan. He was not in any way doing anything that would have undermined Pakistan. As a matter of fact, if Pakistan's—and I've always said this—Pakistan and the United States have a common cause here against terrorism . . . And for them to take this kind of action against somebody who was helping to go after terrorism, I just think is a real mistake on their part."

During the raid the wreckage of a U.S. helicopter was left behind after U.S. Navy Seal Team Six blew up most of it. It became likely through a series of events that Pakistan was allowing representatives of the People's Republic of China [their long-time ally against India] to photograph and take parts of the helicopter. The belief remains that the People's Republic of China used reverse-engineering to dismantle parts in an effort to find out its internal capabilities as well as examination of its stealth skin. On May the 17th of 2011 a little over two weeks after the raid, Pakistan's Prime Minister Gilani went to China for a four day visit.

Next door to Pakistan, in Kabul, Afghanistan came a September 10, 2011 attack killing five Afghans and 77 NATO troops, and [starting on September the 13th of 2011] a 19 hour attack on the U.S. Embassy and NATO Headquarters. According to many officials of the U.S. government who preferred to be anonymous, the attacks had been accomplished in association with the ISI of Pakistan. One who did not choose anonymity was the U.S. Chairman of the Joint Chiefs of Staff, Admiral Mike Mullen who charged Pakistan's ISI with complicity in the attacks. Six days after the 19 hour attack came a third attack, this one on the annex of the U.S. Embassy.

Almost simultaneous with these events came an incident regarding Pakistan's Ambassador to the United States, Husain Haqqani, an Ambassador of considerable talents whose appearances on U.S. television, particularly C-SPAN, were praised by both supporters and critics of Pakistan's policies. Unlike most Ambassadors, he was interesting. That, alone, was enough to be unheard of in D.C. No matter an audience's criticisms of Pakistan's policies, they never failed to applaud enthusiastically after any of his performances as there was respect for his ability to make the outrageous decisions of Pakistan appear to be quite logical. That talent of his was one that all Ambassadors would relish to have as their own.

And so it was no surprise that, so absurdly, there would be legal action taken against him back home in Islamabad. He went back home to defend himself against the charge that he had dictated a memo that was critical of Pakistan's military. The details get terribly boring but the consequences rose high above the boredom threshold. He was compelled to live in fear with his lawyer saying that Haqqani felt it necessary to stay inside out of concern that the ISI could take severe steps against him.

In Afghanistan some plans were being made, not chiefly directed by Kabul but by Washington D.C.

President Obama's Administration's attempt to negotiate with the Taliban for a peace agreement, included baiting them by having serious discussions regarding the Taliban's demand for the release of five of their own who were imprisoned at Guantanamo Bay Naval Base. The five had been selected for U.S. release by the Taliban, adding the demand that the five should be sent straight to Afghanistan or to a third country. [Probably Qatar where the Taliban was planning to establish an office.] Those five had been listed by the United States military as enemy combatants, too dangerous to be released.

Although not directing it, there is another party in all this: President of Afghanistan Hamid Karzai [serving since 2004] who was painfully aware of President Obama's timeline for U.S. withdrawal from Afghanistan; painfully aware that the Taliban had no timeline for their withdrawal; painfully aware that his presidency of Afghanistan may be the first victim of the Taliban reaching again for power over the country, and painfully aware that the Taliban would have no empathy for him as a President or as a person unless maybe he could prove his friendship before their takeover.

On May the 1st of 2012 President Obama and President Karzai jointly signed a "Strategic Partnership Agreement", (not a Treaty but an Agreement). In his speech to the nation after signing the nine page agreement, President Obama said, *"The enormous sacrifices of our men and women are not over. But tonight,*

I'd like to tell you how we will complete our mission and end the war in Afghanistan." After that he talked about reductions in troops and his schedule but, importantly, he said, *"complete our mission and end the war"*—not *win* the war. Shortly after that was when he said *"In coordination with the Afghan government, my Administration has been in direct discussions with the Taliban."*

To negotiate with the Taliban gave credibility to the new world-wide suspicion that the United States had not learned what would have been so obvious to have learned: The 20th Century had illustrated that all attempts to negotiate with tyrannies are useless.

They didn't work in 1938 in Munich when the United Kingdom's Prime Minister Neville Chamberlain signed an agreement with Germany's Chancellor Adolph Hitler and proclaimed the agreement gave Great Britain "Peace in our time."

Or in 1939 when Hitler and the Soviet Union's Joseph Stalin signed a Non-aggression Pact. Hitler then attacked the Soviet Union.

Or in 1945 in Yalta when President Roosevelt and Prime Minister Churchill signed the Yalta Agreements with Joseph Stalin of the Soviet Union promising that those countries to come under a Soviet victory would be given democratic governments. Soon they were turned into proxies of the Soviet Union. It took some 47 years to correct that.

Or in 1953 at Panmunjom with North Korea. That was when North Korea was a threat to South Korea alone. Over one-half century later it was a threat to the world.

Or in 1961 between President Kennedy and Chairman Nikita Khrushchev in Vienna over Laos and Berlin. Khrushchev judged him severely and some two months later built the Wall surrounding West Berlin, and put missiles and bombers in Cuba, bringing about the Cuban Missile Crisis of October, 1962.

Or in 1972 when Leonid Brezhnev of the Soviet Union agreed to an Anti-Ballistic Missile Treaty. In violation, the Soviet Union built and deployed a prohibited large phased array radar station near Krasnoyarsk among other violations not revealed until after the Soviet Union became extinct.

Or in 1973 in Paris with North Vietnam signing the Paris Peace Accords in which all provisions of non-aggression were violated by the North Vietnamese, and a paramount violation committed by the United States Congress by disobeying the provision of the Accords that called for U.S. aid to South Vietnam if there was aggression by the North Vietnamese; the Congress denying that aid. Two years and three months later South Vietnam was forced to surrender.

Or in 1991 when the government of Iraq agreed with the U.N. to enforce Iraqi No-Fly Zones subject to inspection by coalition aircraft, and then Iraq fired at those inspecting aircraft. [Throughout the 1990s the United Nations passed a host of resolutions in punishment of Saddam Hussein's government of Iraq, and the U.N. promptly disregarded their own resolutions. They couldn't even negotiate with themselves.]

Or in 1993 when the Oslo Accords were signed on the South Lawn of the White House by Yasser Arafat promising peace in exchange for land. Israel gave land and Arafat, in exchange, gave violent uprisings and terrorism including a second intifada, this one lasting four years starting in 2004.

Or in 1995 in Dayton, Ohio when the government of Serbia signed the Dayton Accords to bring an end to further killings in Bosnia. The killings were moved to Kosovo by Slobodan Milosevic of the Serbian Government.

Tyrannies that don't care about their own citizens surely do not care about honoring their signature with a foreign government. That signature is not perceived by them as an obligation, but perceived by them as a device to maintain their hold and to expand their tyranny.

Unlike the value of negotiating with free nations and among most governments with whom disputes arise, an oppressive and expansionist tyrannical government should not have more than one chance to offer the end of an international dispute. Once such chance fails, unless a free nation can talk with that tyranny about the date, the protocols, and the modalities regarding the ceremonies necessary for an unconditional surrender of the tyranny, "peace talks" are not worthwhile.

What should be done regarding the Taliban if not negotiate?

Win.

Those Americans who in the second decade of the 21st Century said that the U.S. should *leave* Afghanistan, were unwittingly the most credible salespeople for the aims of enemies of the United States. As usual, the enemies played their side well, using American impatience as their chief weapon to achieve victory. Wait and it will come.

First it was liberals saying to get the U.S. out of Afghanistan; then it was a reemergence of isolationists; then it became many who called Afghanistan's tenth year anniversary since U.S. forces came to Afghanistan, the U.S.'s longest war when it wasn't; and then it was even some conservatives who were sick of hearing about unwarranted attacks by Afghan militants against the U.S. military, and sick of President Karzai. But the United States was there for a reason and the reason was certainly not to make Afghan militants love them and it was not to save President Karzai. The United States was there to extinguish al-Qaeda and its sponsor: the Taliban. Not incidental to that was that the U.S. prevented the Taliban's torture of women of Afghanistan who would be forced a return to that way of life if the United States left prematurely.

It is necessary to remember that beyond the border between Afghanistan and Pakistan are Pakistan's double-ties with both the United States and the Taliban. The U.S. points to Pakistan's nuclear weapons as an excuse to tread lightly, but that weakens the stance of the United States as it caves in to psychological extortion.

Unless all elements of Pakistan's government, including the ISI, become true partners against both al-Qaeda and the Taliban, the United States should propose a Mutual Defense Treaty with India; a friend of the United States; the largest democracy in the world; a close neighbor of Afghanistan, and victim of the Mumbai carnage of 2008 from an attack [called India's 9-11] that originated in Pakistan by the terrorist group Lashkar-e-Taiba that has been associated with both al-Qaeda and the Taliban. Additionally, India too, is a nuclear power, and has successfully test launched a long range solid fuel three-stage mobile missile [the Agni-V on April the 18th of 2012] that can travel some 3100 miles away, including any target in the territory of its long time adversaries; the People's Republic of China and, of course, Pakistan.

As for those heroic Pakistanis who aided the CIA of the United States and were subsequently imprisoned in Pakistan for taking part in that CIA partnership, there was a solution to something similar that was faced by President Theodore Roosevelt. Accounts of the time tell that when he was faced with the kidnapping in Morocco of a long time resident of the United States named Perdicaris by a Moroccan chieftain named Raisuli, the President had his Secretary of State John Hay, issue a warning that the U.S. wanted "Perdicaris alive or Raisuli dead." (Theodore Roosevelt did not always "speak softly" while carrying a big stick.) In addition he announced the United States was immediately sending the U.S. Navy to pick up either Perdicaris alive or Rasuli dead; their decision to come from those two choices. Before the ship arrived in Morocco, Raisuli freed Perdicaris.

Admittedly 2012 was not 1904 and President Barack Obama was not President Theodore Roosevelt.

11

ABOVE THE 38th PARALLEL

NORTH KOREA

If there was ever proof of the futility of negotiating with tyrannies, North Korea stands out as the recipient of the Best Performance by a Dictator, not just winning the award for one year but for three generations. [North Korea isn't the real name: the real name is Democratic People's Republic of Korea but it's much too long for people addressing fan letters.] In each year's acceptance speech at the award ceremonies, North Korea graciously thanks the United States for actually believing its sincerity in negotiations.

First, rushing up to the stage to accept the award was Kim Il Sung known at the time as the Great Leader, but when he died in 1994 his title was changed to the Eternal President. His son, Kim Jong Il took over. Before taking over he was known as the

Dear Leader and his new duties meant a title of more maturity so he became the Supreme Leader. He died in 2011 and his son, Kim Jong-un who was known as the General [although not having served in the military] took over and his title was changed to the Great Successor and then elevated to the title of Supreme Commander. [Keep in mind that in the United States President Washington was called President Washington when he was President, and then after he died he was called President Washington. North Korea has a much more skillful system in the advancement of public prestige.]

North Korean leaders continued to be just as skillful in their acting ability as they were in their titles. Immediately after taking office as the Great Successor, Kim Jong-un indicated that he was open to participation in re-started Six Party Talks to discuss North Korea's nuclear, missile, and other issues of North Korea's military arsenal, as well as non-military areas of concern. [The six parties to the talks being the United States, South Korea, North Korea, Russia, Japan, and as a participant and host, the People's Republic of China.] The Obama Administration was thrilled with the possibility of the Six Party Talks restarting. The State Department enthusiastically started contingency preparations for negotiations.

North Korea has a history of wasting everybody's time in the pursuit of making bad deals. Prime among its deceptions was the 1994 Agreed Framework between the United States of America and the Democratic People's Republic of Korea. That agreement called for North Korea to freeze its nuclear weapons program and allow inspections by the International Atomic Energy Agency [IAEA]. In exchange the United States, Japan, and South Korea would then provide two light-water nuclear plants that were "proliferation-resistant" to replace its graphite-moderated nuclear plants. The agreement had been initiated months earlier by private citizen but former President Jimmy Carter who went to Pyongyang, North Korea, and had two days of discussions with President Kim Il Sung. Eight years later, in 2002, North Korean officials admitted that during those eight years they had been engaged in a clandestine program of uranium enrichment that could be used to build nuclear weapons, and in 2003 North Korea expelled the IAEA inspectors. In a 2003 discussion with the United States and China in Beijing, North Korean officials said they now possessed nuclear weapons.

The fuel rods from the reactor were to have been packaged and shipped out of the country. Instead they extracted the plutonium from the rods and built bombs with it.

It should also be known what kind of offers North Korea makes with consistency across the negotiating table: Since their admitted deception in 1994, North Korea said it would agree to Four Party Talks—there were just four in those days—if the U.S. would give North Korea an additional 100,000 tons of food. The U.S. said yes. That year the U.S. wanted to look for the remains of Americans missing in action. North Korea said the U.S. would have to pay $100,000 per search mission. The U.S. said yes. The same year North Korea demanded South Korea pay North Korea $20,000 to $50,000 for any visit of families from across the border. South Korea said yes. (It would take over 1,000 years at the rate North Korea allowed.)

In 1998 North Korea said it would freeze its missile exports for one billion dollars a year. The United States didn't answer. The same year South Koreans wanted to visit a sacred site in

North Korea and North Korea agreed if South Korea paid millions of dollars in fees over six years. Hyundai said it would pay.

In 1999 the United States wanted to inspect North Korea's underground nuclear site and the U.S. was told they would then have to pay 300 million dollars. The U.S. said yes. In combination with that, the U.S. gave its annual 500,000 tons of food to North Korea in addition to 300,000 tons through the World Food Program. As usual, all evidence is that its recipients were those in the highest echelons of the North Korean government, the military, and the friends of government officials.

In 2000, for another inspection of that nuclear site in Yongbyon, the U.S. gave an additional 100,000 more tons of food and 200,000 more from the World Food Program. That year South Korea wanted to know if relatives in North Korea were dead or alive since mail, phone calls, and other communications were prohibited by North Korean authorities. North Korea was told they would supply the information in return for 1,000 computers paid off in 300 computers a year. (Determination unknown.) That was the year that North Korea said it would stop missile tests if the U.S. would launch satellites for them. [They said nothing about stopping their building and sending their missiles for export to Iran and Syria.] The U.S. did not agree.

In 2010 North Korea demanded 65 *trillion* dollars from the United States for "60 years of hostility." [Who could reject a good deal like that?]

In 2012, North Korea agreed to impose a moratorium on both nuclear tests and long-range missile tests if the United States would restore aid of 240,000 metric tons of food to North Korea. [February the 29th.] The United States endorsed that.

The following week U.S. Senator John Kerry met in New York with Ri Yong Ho, North Korea's nuclear envoy. Senator Kerry announced that "They said that they will live by the agreement they made last week—that we can count on that."

The U.S. could not count on that. The agreement lasted two weeks and two days when on March the 16th North Korea announced it would have a rocket launch of an Unha-3 satellite which would mean a TaepoDong-2 long-range missile test since both require the same launch vehicle. [The difference between a missile and a rocket as hardware is nothing more than one of semantics dependent largely on eventual trajectory and what payload is put under the nosecone of a higher stage above the same launch vehicle. It can be a satellite or a warhead.] North Korea further announced that the satellite would be launched sometime during mid-April to celebrate the 100th anniversary of the birth of the Eternal President, Kim Il Sung; Kim Jong-un's grandfather. North Korea was warned that if it should go ahead with the launch, the United States would cancel the food aid since that was offered on condition that North Korea would not stage any nuclear tests or long-range missile tests. North Korea continued to say it would go ahead with the launch. South Korea and Japan both responded by calling military alerts.

On April the 12th of 2012 the launch took place. No matter its objective, it fell short since it blew up in 90 seconds and its first stage fell into the sea.

Because North Korea made the launch in violation of its agreement with the United States, the U.S. said the food-aid would not be sent. North Korea's response was that it would invoke "retaliatory measures" and "the United States would be held accountable for all the ensuing consequences." It was North Korea's third missile failure, but those in the west who laughed and ridiculed those failures apparently had no memory of the many missile failures in the United States before achieving a successful test flight of an Intercontinental Ballistic Missile. Each test-flight's failure gave data and other information needed for an eventual success.

With a history of more than five decades of talks in one way or another since they started in 1953, the positive results of those talks have been less than zero.

Any agreement made with North Korea could well be more harmful to the United States than not having any agreement at all since the North Korean government has no hesitancy to sign an international agreement without having any intention of keeping it. They are bound to use time and temporary rapport gained in future Six Party Talks or other negotiations for the advancement of their military; to correct errors in their missile technology; and to increase the weight, potency, and number of their nuclear warheads.

Beyond the time used by North Korea to become a greater international threat, is the time that it is given to that government to continue its imposition of terror upon its own people with policies that rank with the greatest horrors of world history. It is a nation where, without exaggeration, the end of each pregnancy is a summons to slavery for the newborn.

U.S. General Mark Clark wrote of his duty in 1953 at the cease-fire armistice agreement between North and South Korea at Panmunjom on the 38th Parallel: "In carrying out the instructions of my government, I gained the unenviable distinction of being the first United States Army commander in history to sign an armistice without victory."

The repercussions have not yet ended.

THE ROLE OF THE PEOPLE'S REPUBLIC OF CHINA

The governments of the People's Republic of China and North Korea were boyhood friends. Both governments came into power just before the 1940s were done; North Korea in 1948 and the People's Republic of China in 1949. They have been partners ever since in both war and peace, with both governments sharing a great deal in common in committing extreme human rights violations against their own people. When North Korea crossed the 38th parallel between North and South Korea, the People's Republic of China joined to help their attempted conquest of South Korea. Over 36,000 Americans were killed in defending South Korea.

Believing in the myth that the People's Republic of China would be a sober influence on North Korea, the United States has been part of Six Party Talks since they started and ended multiple times throughout most of the first decade of the 21st Century.

Although it is not mentioned, the government of the People's Republic of China's reward for its role in hosting the Six-Party Talks is the hope of ultimately intoxicating the United States into feeling obligated to give in to a policy of reciprocity when the People's Republic of China makes its move toward its obsession: the takeover of Taiwan.

The People's Republic of China, at this writing has a minimum of 1,450 missiles targeted at Taiwan from across the Taiwan Strait. Their likely objective is to take jurisdiction of Taiwan prior to 2047 when Hong Kong loses its Special Administrative Region status [S.A.R.] and becomes an integral part of China. In the interim, Hong Kong's status of quasi-independence from China serves as a seduction for Taiwan to become an S.A.R. like Hong Kong and also serves to further an international belief that China is degrading its own authoritarian system. Despite its tremendous inroads into the African and South American continents, and its continual build up of its military, that government wants to cast the impression that there is nothing to fear from the People's Republic of China.

12

ROTATING OBAMA'S GLOBE ACROSS THE PACIFIC BACK TO THE WESTERN HEMISPHERE

HONDURAS

Iran's President Mahmoud Ahmadinejad made a solidarity tour through four nations of Latin America in January of 2012: Venezuela, Nicaragua, Cuba and Ecuador, whose governments all opposed the United States. That was their solidarity. If President Obama had his way three years earlier, for sure there would have been a fifth country on Ahmadinejad's 2012 itinerary: Honduras.

During President Obama's first year in the White House there was a crisis in Honduras; a country with a long time friendship with the United States, particularly noteworthy during President Reagan's administration giving covert and overt help against proxies of the Soviet Union in the Central American War. But that was a long time ago.

It was now many presidents later in both countries, and during the Obama Administration in the United States there was a leftist President of Honduras, Jose Manuel Zelaya, who wanted to stay in office beyond his nation's constitutional limitation of Presidents having no more than one term. Zelaya called for a public referendum to be held to abolish that rule. The act of the President calling for a referendum was also unconstitutional as only the National Congress was granted the authority to call for national referendums. However, at Zelaya's request, Hugo Chavez's government of Venezuela had the ballots printed and shipped to Honduras.

The Honduran Supreme Court, without dissent, ruled Zelaya's actions unconstitutional and directed the nation's military commander, General Romeo Vasquez Velasquez to order Zelaya to leave office. Velasquez did that. When Zelaya was given the order, Zelaya fired General Velasquez and then had a militant group of more than one hundred people break into the compound at the Tegucigalpa Airport in which the ballots had been stored and then, as ordered by Zelaya, the ballots were brought to the Presidential Palace.

All of this was done in defiance of the Constitution, the Supreme Court, the vast majority of the National Congress including his own party, the Attorney General, the Catholic Church, and organizations of the business community.

The Supreme Court directed that the army see to it that Zelaya was removed from office and put under arrest. The army removed him from office but did not imprison him. Instead the army transported Zelaya to exile in Costa Rica. Once done, the

National Congress of Honduras, in keeping with the Constitution of Honduras, appointed the then-current President of the National Congress, Roberto Micheletti, to be Acting President of the Nation until the next constitutionally prescribed election would take place in November.

Supporting all of this were, again, the chief elements of democracy in Honduras as mentioned above. Opposing all of this was the government of Castro's Cuba, the Chavez government of Venezuela and the Obama administration of the United States of America.

President Obama said, *"We believe that the coup was not legal and that President Zelaya remains the President of Honduras; the democratically elected President there."*

Secretary of State Hillary Clinton said that *"the action taken against Honduran President Zelaya violates the precepts of the Inter-Democratic Charter, and thus should be condemned by all."*

The U.S. State Department suspended most foreign aid, suspended regular joint military operations, continued reference to Zelaya as the President, and President Obama supported expulsion of Honduras from the Organization of American States, saying that *"It would be a terrible precedent if we start moving backwards into the era in which we are seeing military coups as a means of political transition rather than democratic elections."*

But a military coup is defined as the military taking over a country rather than handing the reins to a civilian government under the rules and procedures established by the nation's constitution. Moreover, the transitional Acting President Micheletti significantly took himself out of being a presidential candidate.

The election took place as prescribed and Porfirio Lobo was elected President of Honduras on November the 29th of 2009.

Constitutional democracy in Honduras was the winner. Castro, Chavez, and Obama were the losers.

CANADA

It appeared to be a God-send or a Canada-send or maybe both: During a time of an energy crisis came a friendly government with oil and a proposal: Prime Minister Stephen Harper offered a pipe-line of crude oil to run from northern Alberta in Canada all the way down to refineries in the Gulf Coast of Texas. It would mean some 830,000 barrels of oil a day for the United States plus somewhere around 20,000 U.S. jobs. [The figure of 830,000 barrels a day comes from the State Department's Keystone XL Project statement, "The proposed project could transport up to 830,000 barrels per day and is estimated to cost $7 billion. If permitted, it would begin operation in 2013, with the actual date dependent on the necessary permits, approvals, and authorizations."]

Since the oil would be coming from Canada, this came under the foreign policy domain of the President of the United States. It would be up to President Obama to authorize a permit.

After over three years of study and delay including massive opposition by environmental groups came a direct statement from President Obama: *"Earlier today,* [January 18, 2012] *I received the Secretary of State's recommendation on the pending application for the construction of the Keystone XL Pipeline. As the State Department made clear last month, the rushed and arbitrary deadline insisted on by Congressional Republicans prevented a full assessment of the pipeline's impact, especially the health and safety of the American people, as well as our environment. As a result, the Secretary of State has recommended that the application be denied. And after reviewing the State Department's report, I agree."*

At this writing it is difficult to know whether the State Department's recommendation of denial came before or after the President's decision of denial and it may never be known.

All of this seemed to give confirmation to a much earlier [2008] statement of Stephen Chu, President Obama's nominee as his Secretary of Energy, when in a meeting with the Editorial Board of the *Wall Street Journal*, Chu said, "Somehow we have to figure out how to boost the price of gasoline to the levels in Europe."

This policy seemed to be confirmed on February the 28th of 2012 when Representative Alan Nunnelee in House Appropriation Hearings asked Secretary of Energy Chu if the overall goal was to get the U.S. price of gasoline back down, and Chu answered, "No. The overall goal is to decrease our dependency on oil, to build and strengthen our economy."

Six weeks later [March 13, 2012] during a period in which gasoline prices were rising fast, Senator Mike Lee, at a hearing of the Senate Energy and Natural Resources Committee, questioned Secretary Chu about his earlier remarks concerning boosting the price of gasoline. Secretary Chu said, "I no longer share that view."

Perhaps the most difficult to understand answer—even the most difficult to be read—regarding the issue of energy policy was a statement Barack Obama made to the Editorial Board of the *San Francisco Chronicle* during his presidential campaign when he said: *"The problem is, can you get the American people to say this is really important, and force their representatives to do the right thing? That requires mobilizing a citizenry. That requires getting them understanding what is at stake. You know—and climate change is a great example. You know, when I was asked earlier about the issue of coal—you know—under my plan of a cap and trade system, electricity rates would necessarily skyrocket. Even—you know—regardless of what I say about whether coal is good or bad—because I'm capping greenhouse gasses, coal power plants, you know, natural gasses, you name it, whatever the plants were, whatever the industry was, they would have to retrofit their operations. That will cost money. They will pass that money onto consumers."*

Even though President Obama opposed drilling in Alaska [ANWAR: the Arctic Wildlife Refuge in Alaska] as well as limiting oil from shale; opposed off-shore oil drilling from the east and west coasts and the eastern Gulf of Mexico; opposed on-shore federal land drilling; opposed hydraulic fracturing (fracking) for natural gas; opposed coal-fired power plants; on March the 19th of 2011 he told the people of Brazil at a CEO Business Summit in Brasilia, *"We want to work with you. We want to help with technology and support to develop these oil reserves safely, and when you're ready to start selling, we want to be one of your best customers."*

The more current denial of the Canadian Keystone XL Pipeline permit left Canada's Prime Minister Harper in a difficult position. Even his agreement to move the pipeline from areas contested by U.S. environmentalists in Nebraska had been received by a "not now" from the State Department. It seemed that his new proposal would start the whole permit application to be reviewed again all the way from the beginning of the process as though the preceding years of study never took place.

The same day as the President made his statement regarding the denial of a permit for the pipeline, there was a briefing regarding the denial at the State Department in which Kerri-Ann Jones, Assistant Secretary of State [for Oceans and International Environmental and Scientific Affairs], answered questions of the press:

Q. I'm still a little puzzled here. If TransCanada comes back to you with the same route except modifying it to meet its agreement with the state of Nebraska to go around the Ogallala Aquifer, why would you have to review the entire route rather than just the change?

A. Because it would be—it would be a new application for a permit. And as I've said, we are—what's happening today is the permit that is currently pending is being denied, and so a new permit application would trigger a new process. We would certainly, as I stated, look to the information that's out there to the extent we can, but I—it's a new permit application so the process has to be started over again . . .

Q. I'm puzzled as well. I know that the U.S. has made a very big platform of ensuring its energy security. It strikes me that the TransCanada XL pipeline, the Keystone pipeline, would achieve that. So how can you be opining that this is not in the national interest when it goes against this notion of national—of securing your energy future?

A. The determination that's being made today is based on the fact that we have insufficient information at this point. It goes back to the decision that we made on November 10th when we stated that we needed additional information to really—to really determine if this could be in the national interest. And that is why we cannot at this point go forward, because we don't have that information . . .

Q. Do you have specific estimates of how much oil you're foregoing? And when you talk about the national interest, what do you say to those who say that energy independence and our reliance on Iran and other unreliable sources in the global market is a much larger threat than this pipeline would be?

A. Well, I think I would refer you to some of the work that was done in the analysis of the—in the SEIS, where there was analysis in terms of the impact of this pipeline being built or not being built in terms of crude oil coming into the country. And also I think this decision today doesn't make our commitment to energy independence and energy security any less of a priority. It's a major priority for our country. We're making this decision because of the process; we did not have the information we need to make the decision that we thought would be well-informed.

Q. It's still—I guess a lot of us are confused as to how that information could not have been achieved in the weeks that you've had. You were aware of the Nebraska problem for quite some time.

A. Well, it was on November 10th that we made the decision that we needed the additional information, and since then we have been engaged with discussions with the applicant and with the state of Nebraska. At the end of November, I—or towards the end of November, I believe, the state of Nebraska did pass some legislation regarding rerouting, and we have been working on this. But it is a very—it is a complex issue. Looking for alternative routes and identifying them requires a level of specificity and detail that you have to get into to really be able to analyze them, to compare them. And so it is difficult to get the kind of information that we believe is needed to make a very well-informed decision for the country about this, and we didn't—we knew we could not get that done in the 60-day timeline.

Of course not.

Admidst tremendous controversy regarding the decision to deny the permit for the Keystone Pipeline, President Obama announced [March the 22nd of 2012] that "Today we're making this new pipeline from Cushing to the Gulf a priority." Cushing? That is the southern-most link of Keystone from Cushing, Oklahoma to the Gulf Coast; that link to the Gulf being totally domestic, therefore not requiring a presidential permit and that link had already been in the works without problem because it *didn't* require a State Department president-approved permit. The major part of the Keystone pipeline was originating in Canada, crossing an *international* border so indeed, requires presidential approval, which was not given by President Obama.

Notice that denying the permit for Keystone, the State Department's spokesperson said "it is a complex issue." Whenever someone in government uses the word "complex" to describe what it is they're talking about, it is a way of suggesting that they understand the issue but the one to whom they are talking just doesn't have the brainpower. In truth, nothing in governmental affairs is complex except for those subjects that have intentionally been made complicated so others give up trying to give an opposing view. (The areas of U.S. policy that take the most prominence in having been made intentionally complicated are the big three: the U.S. Federal Budget, the Federal Tax Code, and U.S. policy toward China.)

What is easily understood and not complex at all is that Prime Minister Harper of Canada was justifiably upset and would probably send the 830,000 barrels of oil a day and the 20,000 jobs to somewhere other than the United States.

13

ABOVE THE GLOBE: REVERSING KENNEDY'S QUEST OF SPACE SUPREMECY

PRESIDENT OBAMA'S NEW Administrator of the National Aeronautics and Space Administration was being interviewed by Al Jazeera in which, in part, he was asked about the instructions given to him by President Obama. Administrator Charles Bolden answered, "When I became the NASA Administrator—or before I became the NASA Administrator he charged me with three things: One was he wanted me to help re-inspire children to want to get into science and math; he wanted me to expand our international relationships; and third and perhaps foremost he wanted me to find a way to reach out to the Muslim world and engage much more with dominantly Muslim nations to help them feel good about their historic contributions to science and math and engineering." [June 30th of 2010]

Those directives would be called in governmental terms, an extraordinary *change of mission* from the quest outlined by President Kennedy who escalated space exploration into a national pursuit. President Kennedy said: *"No nation which expects to be the leader of other nations can expect to stay behind in this race for space... The eyes of the world now look into space, to the moon and to the planets beyond, and we have vowed that we shall not see it governed by a hostile flag of conquest, but by a banner of freedom and peace....Many years ago the great British explorer George Mallory, who was to die on Mount Everest, was asked why did he want to climb it. He said, 'Because it is there.' Well, space is there and we're going to climb it. And the moon and the planets are there, and new hopes for knowledge and peace are there. And, therefore, as we set sail, we ask God's blessing on the most hazardous and dangerous and greatest adventure on which man has ever embarked."*

Less than four years before John Kennedy became President of the United States an extraordinary and frightening event occurred. It was October the 4th of 1957 during the heart of the Cold War, when the Soviet Union launched the first human-made satellite in world history: Sputnik One. Within the United States, people looked up at the sky at dusk when radio reports told where to look to see that speck of light of the Soviet satellite crossing above U.S. territory. While people were confused and scared at the thought of that sight in the sky, there was a more intense concern at the Department of Defense that had the duty to insure the constitutional function of providing for the common defense. By virtue of the size and weight of the satellite there was no mistaking that whatever rocket launched that satellite was capable of being an Intercontinental Ballistic Missile (ICBM). It was then likely that the Soviet Union had the capability to launch a nuclear warhead that could strike the

United States from the Soviet Union in about 32 minutes from time of launch.

The U.S. had launched its first flight test of an ICBM four months earlier on June 11 of 1957 that had been planned to go downrange from Florida's Air Force Missile Test Center [AFMTC] at Cape Canaveral into the Atlantic Ocean. Instead, 24 seconds into the flight, the destruct button had to be pressed by the Range Safety Officer, blowing it up with most of its pieces landing on the Cape. It was done to prevent Atlas Missile 4A from crashing just south of the Cape into the populated city of Cocoa Beach, Florida.

Another Atlas ICBM, the 6A, was tested in a launch the following September the 25th and also had to be destroyed in flight.

In short, Sputnik One meant the Soviet Union had an ICBM that worked and the United States didn't.

To add insult to injury, it was the International Geophysical Year in which nations of the world had various assignments from the U.N. with the U.S. having been assigned the launch of the world's first human-made satellite. The Soviet Union didn't have that assignment. It now had that prestige while the United States was repeatedly failing not only with its ICBM launch vehicle but with its Vanguard Rocket that was built solely for the purpose of launching a small satellite.

That was the beginning of one Soviet achievement after another while the United States organized the National Aeronautics and Space Agency in 1958. On April the 12th of 1961 the Soviet Union launched Yuri Gagarin who made an orbit of the earth, followed on August the 6th of 1961 with a 17 orbit flight of Gherman Titov.

During the four-month interval between Gagarin and Titov, the United States launched Alan Shepherd on May the 5th of 1961 on a Redstone Rocket—not into orbit at all, and not with a booster capable of being an ICBM but Shepherd was on a flight sending him up and down to test the ability to launch a man into space. It was a flight of 19 minutes. That success in the Mercury capsule Shepherd had named Freedom 7, however small in contrast with Soviet space achievements, received the relief and praise of the nation.

The new President, John F. Kennedy, living through the celebration and spirit of the country and the thrill of it himself as he watched the launch on television in the Oval Office with Vice President Johnson, took an unusual step. Twenty days after the successful launch and recovery of Alan Shepherd, President Kennedy gave a "Second State of the Union Address" titled *Special Message to the Congress on Urgent National Needs* to a Joint Session of the Congress stating: *"The Constitution imposes upon me the obligation to 'from time to time give to the Congress information on the state of the union.' While this has traditionally been interpreted as an annual affair, this tradition has been broken in extraordinary times. These are extraordinary times."* He went on to propose a number of initiatives including additional spending for a stronger defense beyond what he had proposed in his original State of the Union Address that he gave on January the 30th, but then he added something unprecedented: *"I believe this nation should commit itself to achieving the goal, before this decade is out of landing a man on the moon and returning him safely to earth."*

Shortly after that, in the blockhouse of Pad 14 at Cape Canaveral used for Atlas Missiles, there was an informal meeting of some of the most brilliant space technicians and scientists in the nation. They were eating sandwiches from the "Gaggin' Wagon" that visited the pads at lunchtime and they were talking about what they had to do to get an Astronaut to the moon before the end of the decade, little more than eight years away. They were scheduling inventions. They were giving dates when things that did not already exist, must exist. Without their scheduled inventions, the President's deadline would be missed. They had to invent some items by July of 1961, and invent any number of things by April of 1962, others by November of 1962, others by March of 1963, and on, and on.

On the wall above a panel of buttons in the blockhouse was a sign that read, "Man will never reach the moon regardless of all future scientific advances...Lee DeForest, 1957." And there was a big X mark covering it, the mark made with a red grease pencil, but the words beneath it were still intentionally readable. Below it was the same red of the grease pencil with the written words, "Oh, yeah?"

By the dedication of the President and the nation and the successful creativity, genius, and scheduling of literally hundreds of inventions, and of two following Presidents; Johnson and Nixon, the goal was achieved with over five months to spare before the *"decade was out."*

In 1962 President Kennedy had said, *"To be sure—we are behind, and will be behind for some time in manned flight. But we do not intend to stay behind, and in this decade we shall make up and move ahead."*

The United States won the race for space.

On September the 22nd of 2011, Neil Armstrong, the first man in the history of the world to walk on the moon and also one of the most humble celebrities in the history of the world, came out of virtual self-imposed public seclusion to give a rare appearance before the U.S. House of Representatives Committee of Commerce, Science, and Technology to state his opposition to President Obama's decisions canceling launches of previously scheduled flights of Astronauts on U.S. vehicles. Among the cuts President Obama made was the termination of the Constellation project with the Ares rocket and the Orion crew-capsule for voyages of Astronauts going back to the moon with prospective longer range missions to Mars. The following are excerpts from the testimony of Neil Armstrong:

"For a country that has invested so much for so long to achieve a leadership position in space exploration and exploitation, this condition is viewed by many as lamentably embarrassing and unacceptable . . .

"More than 60 countries are investing in space. China has sent Taikonauts into orbit and tells of their plans to fly to the moon. India is planning human space flight. Cargo to the International Space Station is flown on Russian, Japanese, or European craft. Americans currently have no access to space on American rockets or in American spacecraft...

"Most importantly, public policy must be guided by the recognition that we live in a technology driven world where progress is rapid and unstoppable . . . Our choices are to lead, to try to keep up, or get out of the way. A lead, however earnestly and expensively won, once lost, is nearly impossible to regain . . .

"The absence of a master plan that is understood and supported by government, industry, academia and society as a whole frustrates everyone. NASA itself, driven by conflicting forces and the dashed hopes of canceled programs, must find ways of restoring hope and confidence to a confused and disconsolate work force. The reality that there is no flight requirement for a NASA pilot-Astronaut for the foreseeable future is obvious and painful to all who have, justifiably, taken great pride in NASA's wondrous space flight achievements during the past half century.

"Winston Churchill famously stated: 'The Americans will always do the right thing after they have exhausted all the alternatives.' In space flight, we are in the process of exhausting alternatives. I am hopeful that, in the near future, we will be doing the right thing."

On the same date and to the same House Committee, Commander Eugene Cernan, the last man to have walked on the moon, submitted his testimony in writing to that House Committee:

"Lest we forget, Mr. Chairman, it was a bold and courageous President over a half century ago who started us on a journey to the stars—a journey from which America would never look back—and a journey that challenged the American people at every crossroad to do what most thought couldn't be done . . . And, it was not going to be easy, but hard, and did require sacrifice, just as John F. Kennedy said it would. However, being second best was unacceptable then, and being just good today is never going to be good enough for the American people.

"JFK did not just challenge us to go to the moon—he

believed it was time to take a leading role in space—a role he thought might well hold the key to our future on Earth. So we built upon the uncertainty of Mercury, fabricated Gemini, the bridge to Apollo, and then realized the dream of mankind for eons of time when over 40 years ago we were able to call the moon our home . . .

"Along the way, thousands of young Americans, who, inspired by what was happening around them, became doctors, engineers, teachers, scientists, and even university Presidents—a 'stimulus' for education unparalleled in our history...

"However, today we are on a path of decay. We are seeing the book closed on five decades of accomplishments as the world's leading space-faring nation. As unimaginable as it seems, we have now come full circle and ceded our leadership role in space back to the same country, albeit with a different name, that spurred our challenge five decades ago . . .

"We eventually need an Administration that believes in and understands the importance of America's commitment to regaining its preeminence in space; an administration which will provide us with a leader who will once again be bold and challenge our people to do what history has now told us is possible . . .

"The short-term solution is more complex in light of NASA and the present Administration's now obvious agenda to dismantle a space program that has been five decades in the making. First on this agenda was to cancel Constellation—a $10 billion investment five years in development. Embedded in the Constellation architecture was the culture of a long-range building block that could not only service the ISS, extend the life of Hubble, provide national security, but additionally would be capable of carrying us back to the moon and on to Mars. To replace Constellation was a 'mission to nowhere'...

"'Mission to Somewhere' logically points to the moon, thereby building the foundation for a voyage to Mars. Unfortunately, it might well be a generation or more before the U.S. once again exerts its influence in Space Exploration beyond Earth orbit. 'If we don't know where we are going, we might end up where we are headed'...

"Very little if anything has changed my assessment of the Administration's space policy since my testimony before this Committee over a year ago. I recounted the words of my colleagues and myself in describing the Administration's plan for the future of Space Exploration—'Devastating', 'Slide to mediocrity', 'Third-rate stature', 'Mission to nowhere.'...

"Those best and brightest minds at NASA and throughout the multitudes of private contractors, large and small, did not join the team to design windmills or redesign gas pedals, but to live their dreams of once again taking us where no man has gone before...

"We are at a crossroad. If we abdicate our leadership in space today, not only is human spaceflight and space exploration at risk, but I believe the future of this country and thus the future of our children and grandchildren as well. Now is the time for wiser heads in the Congress of the United States to prevail. Now is the time to overrule this Administration's pledge to mediocrity. Now is the time to be bold, innovative and wise in how we invest in the future of America. Now is the time to re-establish our nation's commitment to excellence."

"Mr. Chairman, Ladies and Gentlemen—it is not about space—it's about the country.

"Thank you for your time and patience.

"Sincerely, and with respect,

"Eugene A. Cernan

"Commander, Apollo XVII"

Less than five months after the testimonies of Neil Armstrong and Eugene Cernan came the submission from President Obama of the budget for Fiscal Year 2013 in which it was revealed the cutting of funds that would result in even more future cancellations in space exploration including the termination of NASA's ExoMars Robotic Spaceflight Program which had been a joint effort of the U.S. and the European Space Agency. It was designed to robotically gather samples of Mars and return the samples to earth. Manned launches were out as of the previous year's budget, and now the key unmanned launch was also being cancelled.

At Rice University on September the 12th of 1962, President Kennedy gave a major address on the U.S. commitment to the quest of outer space, and said: *"I realize that this is in some measure an act of faith and vision, for we do not now know what benefits await us."*

At this writing it is five decades later and during those five decades we learned what benefits awaited us: advances and inventions including medical imaging devices, radiation hazard detectors, self-righting life rafts, air quality monitors, virtual reality devices, water purification systems, ultrasound systems, computer elements by the hundreds, heart pacemakers, voice controlled wheelchairs, fire resistant materials, radiation insulation, scratch resistant lenses, memory chips, telling the differences between malignant or benign tumors without surgery, inflatable antennas for remote areas and for disaster zones, image sensors used in cell phone cameras, and weather forecasting far in advance of what was able to be predicted previously.

NASA called that list, including more than 1700 items, "spin-off benefits" of the U.S. space program. But that list had much more importance than the implication of the name, "spin-offs." They are better described as vast improvements in the quality of life and even the length of lives with numbers beyond estimation.

In addition to all this, space exploration has added countless benefits to the defense of the nation since space exploration and military significance is interlocked. President Reagan's Strategic Defense Initiative was so feared by the Soviet Union that it was instrumental in the Soviets losing the Cold War.

As for the future, *"we do not now know what benefits await us"* if the United States would continue the pursuit of space exploration without cutting arteries in its life-blood.

If President Kennedy's passion for U.S. superiority in space exploration continues to be rejected by President Obama or by forthcoming Presidents of the United States, all that will be left will be the hope that the leaders in space will be the European Space Agency, India, Japan and South Korea, rather than having the leadership taken by Russia, China, North Korea, and Iran.

14

BACK HOME:
DOWNGRADING
THE COMMON DEFENSE:

"Opinions of America are higher than they've been in years. Yes, the world is changing; no we can't control every event. But America remains the one indispensible nation in world affairs—and as long as I'm President, I intend to keep America that way. That's why, working with our military leaders, I have proposed a new defense strategy that ensures we maintain the finest military in the world, while saving nearly half a trillion dollars in our budget."

President Barack Obama
Beginning his Fourth Year in Office
Third State of the Union Address
January the 24th of 2012

Two days later, on January the 26th the official announcement was made that (against the advice of many U.S. military leaders) within the new federal budget to be submitted by the President to start October the 1st of 2012 [the beginning of Fiscal Year 2013] the purchase of F-35 stealth fighter jets will be slowed; the U.S. Air Force will retire six tactical air squadrons, 89 cargo aircraft, and one training squadron; the U.S. Navy will retire seven cruisers and at least delay purchase of some submarines including the new generation of submarines that would have carried long range nuclear missiles; military pay raises will be slowed down by 2016; the U.S. Marine Corps will reduce 10,000 marines from its force; and the army will reduce its force by 80,000 soldiers. Some of the cuts would be immediate and some in stages through the next ten years.

All of this was for the proposed budget, in addition to the proposed sequestration trigger of the "super-committee" advocated by the President, that could, on the second day of January of 2013, start the reduction of $600 billion more in defense.

[A "super-committee" of 12 members of the Congress had been organized to find $1.2 trillion to cut from all facets of the federal government; half from defense and the other half from the rest of the government, excluding entitlements of Social Security and Medicare. The super-committee announced its failure on November the 21st of 2011. Pending a commensurate cut by the Congress prior to January the 2nd of 2013, the prescribed cuts as outlined for the super-committee's failed charge, would come into automatic effect.]

On November the 2nd of 2011 there was a hearing of the House Armed Services Committee on the sequestration of U.S. defense forces in which General Raymond Odierno, Chief of

Staff of the United States Army testified, "Cuts of this magnitude would be catastrophic to the military."

Admiral Jonathan W. Greenert, Chief of Naval Operations of the United States Navy said, "In my view, sequestration will cause irreversible damage. It will hollow the military and we will be out of balance in manpower—both military and civilian."

General Norton A. Schwartz, Chief of Staff of the United States Air Force said, "We again will be left with a military with aging equipment, extremely stressed human resources with less than adequate training, and ultimately declining readiness and effectiveness . . . We therefore join Secretary Panetta and Chairman Dempsey in advising against across-the-board cuts . . . Ultimately, such a scenario gravely undermines our ability to protect the nation."

The testimony before the committee was long, but that day George Little, Press Secretary of the Department of Defense succinctly condensed the consequences should the projected cuts of sequestration be made. He noted that the United States would then have the smallest Air Force in the history of the service, and the smallest Navy since the Woodrow Wilson Administration.

On November the 21st, 2011, nineteen days after the testimony to the congressional committee was given, President Obama said to reporters in the White House Press Room: *"Already some in Congress are trying to undo these automatic spending cuts. My message to them is simple: No! I will veto any effort to get rid of those automatic spending cuts to domestic and defense spending. There will be no easy off-ramps on this one."*

It should be noted that President Obama said that *"some in Congress are trying to undo these automatic spending cuts."* But surely he knew that the most important dissent came not from those *in* the Congress but from those testifying *to* the Congress, with that testimony coming from those directly engaged in the military readiness of the United States.

The reasoning behind the cuts was that there was an economic crisis and as a result, every department, agency, and bureau of the federal government minus the entitlements mentioned, "have to be cut and there can be no sacred cows" in that cutting. Of course there not only *can* be a sacred cow; there *must* be a sacred cow: the survival of the United States. And in a wider view, the conclusion of this war will determine if civilization as we know it will survive.

The Constitution gives the charge to the federal government to *"provide for the common defense."* That charge should drive the budget; the budget should not drive whether the government will or will not accept that constitutional directive. Just like a person, the stuff of survival for family should drive the home budget, even if it takes two jobs; or even more sacrifice. Purchase of less necessary things that are wanted have to wait for a later time when they can be afforded.

Even as a staunch admirer of FDR, President Obama either unintentionally or intentionally ignored that by the time of the last fiscal year of World War II [that started on July the First of 1944] defense was given 89½% of the United States Budget, leaving only 10½% for *everything else*. [Education and Social Services were 0.14%. Social Security was 0.29%.] All of that 89½% for defense was received without complaint by the vast majority of the people of the United States. Victory was imperative.

Isolationists often argue that providing for the common defense is valid only when it means the United States itself is attacked. Of course that criterion was met on 9-11. But providing the common defense is more than providing it after an attack. Vision demands that a nation recognizes events in the world that will make a coming attack on the United States a likely event. That means there is a time for preemption. Endorsement of preemption was well known throughout the nation for weeks following 9-11, but when the shock was gone, so was that recognition. Americans are uniquely in a hurry to get on to the life they knew rather than recognize life as it has changed.

Having crept into the accepted vocabulary of Americans, "defense spending" is the only item in the U.S. federal budget that is commonly referred to as "spending." No one says, "food stamps spending" or "Social Security spending" or "housing and urban development spending" or "arts and humanities spending" or "education spending" or "infrastructure spending" or "Amtrak spending" or "Corporation for Public Broadcasting spending." Those are programs. Only defense receives that constant reminder by government spokespeople and media that defense costs money as though nothing else does.

Not so incidentally, other than defense, none of those other items mentioned above are in the U.S. Constitution.

Finally, the financial cost of defense is more difficult to estimate than any other item in the budget because so much of defense has to be based on contingencies; those things that *might* happen—and might *not* happen. The U.S. cannot determine the intent of other governments of the world, particularly as those governments change and can move from friendly to hostile in an instant. Programs such as Social Security and Medicare, and so many other items can be estimated based on population, median age, life expectancies, all of which are able to be computed with some foundation. Road maintenance can be calculated on how many interstate highways exist and how much maintenance for them will be necessary.

More foresight is also needed for items of defense than most other items because of the time it takes to produce and deploy a new battleship, a new bomber, new intercontinental ballistic missiles. They are items that cannot be built in one fiscal year or, in some cases, not even in a single decade.

After the demise of the Soviet Union and the success of the liberation of Kuwait in 1991, President Bush (41) did what some other Presidents mistakenly did after wars were won: assume the military should be reduced. He recommended to the Congress a reduction of $50 billion from the military over the following five years. As soon as he made the announcement, Democrat leaders claimed that the reduction should be twice as steep, for a reduction of $100 billion. There was no itemization made in such quick advocacy; it was simply the doubling of the reduction recommended by the President. It was called the "Peace Dividend" and it meant funds that would have been spent on defense should now be moved to domestic issues.

Chairman of the Joint Chiefs of Staff, General Colin Powell, argued back then that "greater cuts [than those that had been recommended by the President] could threaten U.S. readiness." It was just months later that President Clinton came into office and requested even greater reductions. He called for a presidential cut of $72 billion more than President Bush which became a total reduction of $122 billion. That was a total disregard of General Powell's warning that greater cuts beyond those of President Bush could threaten U.S. readiness.

On September 1, 1993, Secretary of Defense Les Aspin justified the trimmed-down military plan of the Clinton Administration by saying that, "We'll have a force based on tomorrow's requirements." It was as though tomorrow was known, despite the absence of any U.S. Department of Prophecy.

There is, however, a U.S. Department of Memory called the Library of Congress:

General Douglas MacArthur wrote on September the 15, of 1941: "The history of failure can be summed up in two words, 'too late.' Too late in comprehending the deadly purpose of a potential enemy. Too late in realizing the mortal danger. Too late in preparedness. Too late in uniting all possible forces for resistance. Too late in standing with ones friends."

On August the 26th and self-paraphrased on September the 6th of 1960, Senator John F. Kennedy said: *"There can be only one possible defense policy for the United States and that is summed up in the word 'first.' I do not mean first 'but'. I do not mean first 'when'. I do not mean first 'if'. I mean first 'period!' Only then can we prevent war by preparing for it."*

President Kennedy had prepared a speech for his delivery in Austin, Texas on November the 22nd of 1963. His assassination that day prevented the delivery of that speech in which he was prepared to say:

"I pledged in 1960 to build a national defense which was second to none—a position I said, which is not 'first but,' not 'first if,' not 'first when' but first—period. That pledge has been fulfilled. In the past three years we have increased our defense budget by over 20 percent;

increased the program for acquisition of Polaris submarines from 24 to 41; increased our Minuteman missile purchase program by more than 75 percent; doubled the number of strategic bombers and missiles on alert; doubled the nuclear weapons available in the strategic alert forces; increased the tactical nuclear forces deployed in Western Europe by 60 percent; added five combat ready divisions and five tactical fighter wings to our Armed Forces; increased our strategic airlift capabilities by 75 percent; and increased our special counter-insurgency forces by 600 percent. We can truly say today, with pride in our voices and peace in our hearts, that the defensive forces of the United States are, without a doubt, the most powerful and resourceful forces anywhere in the world."

In contrast, President Obama and Russia's President Dmitri Medvedev signed a new Strategic Arms Reduction Treaty [April 8th of 2010] significantly reducing the number of nuclear weapons of each side. The new Obama-Medvedev treaty was ratified by the U.S. Senate 71 to 26 [December the 22nd of 2010].

The dangers of the treaty are many, foremost among those dangers is that any agreement with one nation; in this case, Russia, is that other nuclear nations are not subject to its terms. It holds the United States to limits no matter what the People's Republic of China or North Korea or Pakistan may do singularly or collectively in the future, or if one or more supply rogue states their technology and weapons.

That is not to even take into account the many violations the Soviet Union made of its nuclear treaties, with some violations known at the time and more learned after the Soviet Union ended. It is also not to take into account that verification is more than questionable regarding non-deployed missiles; solid fuel mobile missiles can be transported and shielded anywhere for quick launch; parts of missiles that have been disassembled can be reassembled; and it is questionable as to how many Multiple Independently Targeted Reentry Vehicles [MIRVS] are being put underneath nosecones of missiles. In the shadows behind all of this is the knowledge that its leadership wants to regain what it once had under the Soviet Union: the title of a Superpower. The only way the Soviet Union became a superpower from the end of the 1950s into the '60s and the '70s and '80s was due to its military strength. Nothing else. It was not an industrial superpower or an agricultural superpower or a superpower in trade or a superpower in tourism and certainly not a superpower in morality.

Beyond the new treaty, President Obama made overtures of unilateral proposals to cut nuclear weaponry even further than those cuts called for in the treaty, including stopping all testing, which would be tantamount to leaving automobiles built decades back without turning on the ignition during those decades to make sure they still work.

Without the United States nuclear superiority, those nations that counted on the United States as a safeguard will not feel as secure. And those governments hostile to the United States and its allies will feel strengthened as they can increase their nuclear weapons without a contest since the United States had signed a limiting agreement with Russia.

We know that every time any great power has given the perception of military reduction, some other power or powers immediately started to fill the vacuum. Always. Not sometimes, but always. Contemporary history obeyed tradition when President Bush (41) proposed a reduction of $50 billion in our military, taking only days for the People's Republic of China to announce it was increasing its military budget by 13.8%. When President Clinton proposed a further reduction to a total of $122 billion, the People's Republic of China announced it was increasing its military budget by another 15%. What power was threatening China? None. The People's Republic of China was attempting to fill the vacuum that was being created by the United States.

When members of the 103rd Congress agreed to President Clinton's request for steeper defense cuts, they didn't know what was coming in the years ahead. What was coming was 9-11.

The rule that should always be observed is that a "Peace Dividend" is a fool's policy.

Because the United States can rarely, if ever, be visionary enough to be "just right" in the funds appropriated for defense because of all the unknowns of the future, that lack of certain knowledge means that the appropriations will most likely be too much or too little. If too much is spent, then the people of the United States will have wasted a lot of money. If too little is spent, then the people of the United States will have wasted the nation.

Money is expendable. The United States is not.

Al-Zawahiri, the leader of al-Qaeda said, "We will defeat the United States as it was defeated in Vietnam in 1975, and defeated in Lebanon in 1983 and defeated in Somalia in 1993." He knew his history.

Mahmoud Ahmadinejad of Iran said, "We shall soon experience a world without the United States." His superior, the Ayatollah Khamenei said that "The United States will soon be defeated."

The chant shouted on so many far-away streets is "Death to America!" Some Americans, perhaps most Americans, have regarded that as nothing more than talk. Before World War II that's the way "Mein Kampf" was regarded. During those days a member of the House of Commons asked Winston Churchill, "Please explain why you insist on continuing to fight Hitler!"

Churchill answered, "If I stop, you'll find out why."

If the United States stops its world leadership, the world will find out why it shouldn't have stopped. In just the latter half of the 20th Century Americans fought and died for the liberty of strangers including Koreans, Vietnamese, Laotians, Cambodians, Grenadans, Somalians, Bosnians, Kosovars and Kuwaitis. If it is not able to do that in the future, no one will.

Having witnessed or heard of that U.S. history, every Chief of State around the world knows that the United States has the most powerful military in the world with its quality of troops, the advanced technology, and its unparalleled weaponry. But every Chief of State around the world also knows that the United States will not use the power it has. Therefore, the United States is less powerful than those who have fighters with ambitions to be martyrs and have primitive weaponry, having at times chosen airlines in flight as functional missiles in their otherwise 14th century arsenals.

The U.S. does not need to *use* the power of every weapon it has, but the U.S. does need to prove that it is *willing* to use every weapon it has for survival—and mean it. Enemies must fear that the U.S. is not just able, but willing. Fear is the weapon that can prevent potential armed conflicts from becoming reality.

Often with regret, and sometimes with relief, governments, like most things in life, are temporary. The quest of any President of the United States should be to see to it that the United States of America will not, like most things, be temporary. The nation's permanence is the greatest pursuit in human history—because if successful, that success will determine the immortality of those Americans who came before us and will determine the lives and liberties of those at home and around the world who are yet unborn.

EPILOGUE: THE FUTURE

NO MATTER WHEN this book is read, for sure many pertinent events will have taken place since the writing was completed on May the 3rd of 2012 and therefore are left unmentioned in this book.

One known event is that on January the 20th of 2013 there will be an inaugural ceremony above the west steps of the U.S. Capitol Building. It might be the Second Inaugural of Barack Obama or it might be the First Inaugural of someone else. Either way, that elected leader will be a War-Time President.

It is the hope and belief that the President speaking at the ceremony that day will have the wisdom and strength to win the war. Beyond that, the President must have the ability to summon the American people in dedicating themselves to achieve that victory. And most of all, that leadership must insure that the United States of America will endure beyond the markings on the face of any watch or clock or calendar.

INDEX

Political Map of the World, April 2012